SOUTHERN
TALK

SOUTHERN TALK

A Disappearing Language

**RAY
CUNNINGHAM**

Bright Mountain Books, Inc.
Fairview, North Carolina

Printed in the United States of America

ISBN-10: 0-914875-22-1 (*Southern Talk: A Disappearing Language* is a revised and expanded edition of *Old Timey Southern Talk*, ISBN 0-8187-0094-7, published in 1987 by Harlo Press.)
ISBN-13: 978-0-914875-22-2

Library of Congress Cataloging-in-Publication Data

Cunningham, Ray, 1921-
    Southern talk : a disappearing language / Ray Cunningham
        p.   cm.
    Enl. ed. of: Old timey southern talk. 1987.
    ISBN 0-914875-22-1
    1. English language-Dialects-Southern States-Glossaries, vocabularies, etc. 2. English language-Southern States-Terms and phrases. 3. Southern States-Popular culture-Dictionaries. 4. Americanisms-Southern States-Dictionaries. 5. Figures of speech-Dictionaries.   I. Cunningham, Ray, 1921- Old timey southern talk. II. Title.
PE2926.C87 1993
427'.975-dc20
                                                          93-30379

Dedication

To the relatively few Southerners who still talk right, for helping me remember all the beautiful words and phrases found in this book.

Introduction

Talking is, and always has been, the most expressive form of communication. Oral messages can and do convey much more than those that are printed, and they are less likely to be misunderstood because not only do we hear what is being said, we can see it too! Sometimes what we see—hand and body movements or eye and facial expressions—speaks louder than what we hear. The speed, the hesitation, the stammering, the loudness or softness of speech all tell us something of the speaker's meaning as well.

America's early settlers brought with them the languages of their native lands, the most prevalent of which was some form of English. Those who started building towns and cities came in contact with many who spoke different languages or different English dialects. Gradually they all started blending, and a new form of American English emerged.

There were few newspapers, and only a small percentage of the people could read anyway. Town criers did a pretty good job of spreading the news within the towns, and travelers carried news from town to town. Just because something might have happened several weeks ago didn't prevent it from being news, because news has always been what one hears about for the first time.

The farmers, and those who wanted to be, moved on to establish homesteads far from the populated areas. Although these self-sufficient pioneers were, for the most part, even less educated as far as books go, they were, and had to be, very smart in all that is required to become the sole supplier of one's needs. What was considered a very close neighbor was someone who lived a mile or so away, so news traveled very slowly. But for folks who either grew or made almost every-thing they had, there was little need to know about anything else. There was less reason to acquire book learning for this way of life; therefore little was done to promote it.

Since there were few standards for verbal communication, everybody started talking pretty much as they pleased. Some of it was proper, or fairly close to it; some was sort of made up because it sounded good. Over time, some words became shortened, others lengthened, some had the ending letters changed completely, and even the basic sounds of many words were changed. Without common usage, the various regions of the country developed their speech in individual ways.

Something came along in the 1920s which started causing changes in the way people talked. It was radio. For the first time for many, country folk could hear what people from the city sounded like. Most didn't like it at first, perhaps didn't even understand it, but little by little radio talk became accepted. Before long, the silent movies became talkies, and people everywhere found out how to talk to the opposite sex, how to talk show business talk, cowboy talk, bad guy talk, even Tarzan talk (if talking is what he did).

Then along came World War II and people from all over the country, rural and urban, got thrown together for military training. Such funny sounding talk! Some sounded city, some country, some sounded like northerners, some southerners, and the rest were somewhere in between. After the war came television which had the most impact of all on standardizing our language. Television announcers were trained to sound neutral, and eventually everybody started sounding more and more neutral too. Over the years, as the American populace became more educated and the rules of written English were incorporated more fully into the oral language, the old timey talk was seldom.

Part of the charm of regional speech lies in its variety. Pronunciation and vocabulary vary from state to state, from county to county, and sometimes even from neighborhood to neighborhood. I have spent a lifetime listening to the old timey talk in Alabama, Louisiana, Tennessee, North Carolina, South Carolina, Virginia, and Florida during the periods I have lived in each of those states. While there are definite similarities, I've found that there are few rules for southern talk, but it's a little like English, sometimes. This collection of words and phrases is derived from around the whole South, but you won't hear the same kind of talk in each state.

Many of the words or expressions listed here may have been used across the country but their pronunciations make them southern; others are so uniquely tied to their locale as to need translation only a few states away. Certain expressions nearly defy definition, but since their meaning is clear from context, they have been left to stand on their own, often just as I remember some old timer having spoken them.

Old timey southern talk is so much a part of our past that it's saddening to me to see it die out. The examples of words and sayings I've collected over a lifetime will give you have some idea of how I heard southern talk. I only wish it were possible for you to hear for yourself how the old southern folks "talked" it.

Have a good time!

SOUTHERN TALK

◄ A ►

A
A contraction for *have* or *to* when part of a verb.
"I woulda gone but I couldn't git away."

ABIDE
Tolerate, endure; generally used negatively.
"I kain't abide that least young-un of hern."

A BODY
A person, one.
"With all the meanness a-goin' on, it's got to whir a body ain't safe to step out of the house no more."

ACROSS THE WATERS
Overseas.
"Hit never made no sense sendin' our boys across the waters when hit wasn't none of our business."

ACROST
Across.
"We kain't git acrost the creek 'cause it's too deep to ford till it goes down some more."

Overheard . . .
"Witches don't leave no tracks, an' they don't throw no shader neither."

ADDLED
Confused, muddled.
"Grandma-she thought she had killed that-there snake, but she had jist addled it."

AFEARED
Afraid.
"I ain't hardly afeared of nothin' 'cept snakes."

AFOOT
On foot, walking.
"When I seen Abner a-limpin' acrost the field afoot, I knowed that old crazy horse had done throwed him."

AFTER WHILE
After a while.
"Ain't no need to git out in the heat of the day. Why don't you jist wait till after while to pick them beans?"

AGG'AVATE
Aggravate.
"All that boy likes to do is show out an' agg'avate somebody."

AGIN
Again, another time, once more.
"I done told you wunct, don't you do that agin."

AGINST
Against.
"Them big timber people is the ones that's fer it. Ever'body else, as fer as I know, is aginst it."

A-HERE
Here.
"Look a-here at what I'm doin'."

A-HOLT
A hold.
"I kain't git a-holt of her."

AIG
Egg.
"I like me some salt an' pepper on my biled aig."

AIG ON
Egg on, incite.
"If you aig on old Homer enough he'll fight you. He'd fight a buzz saw if he gits riled enough."

AIMIN' TO
Intending to.
"I was aimin' to git that cow milked 'fore night set in."

AINT
Ant; aunt.
"I ain't seen nary aint since Aint Mary learnt me how to git shed of um."

AIN'T ABOVE DOIN' THIS OR THAT
Not too perfect to do whatever the action might be.
"Josh ain't above takin' a little nip wunct in a while."

AIN'T MUCH COUNT
Not very good.
"Here lately my roomatiz has been so bad I jist got to whir I ain't much count fer nothin'."

AIN'T NO FAIR
Isn't fair.
"It ain't no fair to peep till we all git hid."

AIN'T RIGHT, NOT RIGHT
Mentally retarded.
"That oldest boy of Misseries Thigpen's jist ain't right, but there's a heap of thangs he can do fer her anyhow."

AIN'T WORTH A MILK BUCKET UNDER A BULL
Valueless, useless, purposeless.
"Melvin's new coon hound ain't worth a milk bucket under a bull. All he does is trot along right behind Melvin's heels jist like a town dog."

AIN'T WORTH KILLIN'
Of very little value.
"Irene shore got one more sorry man. Why, he ain't worth killin'. I mean, he ain't worth the powder an' lead it'd take to blow him to hell."

AIRISH
Breezy, cool, drafty.
"Hit got perty airish last night an' I had to git up an' shet the winder."

AIRN
Any, one.
"John's got him a dime but I ain't got airn."

AIRS
Errors.
"All them Cardinals done durin' the whole ball game was make airs."

ALL BROKE UP
Distressed over some misfortune.
"Misseries Thornton has been all broke up ever since her cat got drownded in that old well."

ALL-DAY SINGING
AND DINNER ON THE GROUND

All-day singing and dinner on the ground was jist about the biggest church doin's they was. Whichever one of the churches has it, ever'body comes. Hit don't make no nevermind whir they're Church of Gods, Methodists, or Babtistes, er any of um. They'll have some of them real good sangin' quartets and then they'll have jist ever'body to sang and have a big old time.

Jist 'fore dinnertime the womenfolks commences to spreadin' them tablecloths and bedsheets down on the ground in a big long row. You ain't never seen sitch fine vittles in yore born days. It looks like to me that them ladies is tryin' to outcook each other, 'cause ever'thang is so larrupin' good. The preacher jist gits plumb carried away with the thanks and blessin' till ever'body's so hungry that their guts start to growlin'. When he finally gits done with it, you ain't never seen so much bendin' and bobbin' and stoopin' and squattin', gittin' to that grub. Whenever the eatin's done, nearly ever'body's belly is tighter'n a tick, so they kain't git back to sangin' till their dinner settles a while.

ALL FOURS
Hands and knees.
"Bill-he was down on all fours an' the young-uns was playin' like he was a horse an' ridin' him."

ALL HAT AND NO CATTLE
More show than substance.
"Why Junior Ellis ain't got a pot to pee in er a winder to throw it out of; he jist likes to put on the dog. He's all hat and no cattle."

ALL OVER CREATION
Everywhere.
"The teacher went to the World's Fair an' tuck a bunch of pitchers an' showed um to us. I wouldn't go to one of them thangs if somebody paid my way. They was people all over creation."

ALL-OVERS
A strange shivery feeling.
"When I see a chicken with his head wrung off a-jumpin' and a-flappin' and a-squirting blood ever'whir, I jist git the all-overs."

ALL SPRUCED UP
All cleaned up and dressed up.
"Ernie allus gits all spruced up when he goes to town, figures he might find him a gal."

ALL THE GO
In vogue, fashionable, popular.
"Bobbed hair is gittin' to be all the go."

ALLUS
Always.
"I allus go to town on Saturday evenin' to git stuff fer the old woman."

ALL VINES AND NO TATERS
Much less than appearance suggests.
"Aubry likes to spout off about all he knows and all the stuff he's got, but I'll tell you what I know: he's all vines and no taters."

ALTER
Castrate.
"Whenever the moon gits right, I'm gonna alter them-there shoats an' have us a big mess of mountain oysters."

AMBEER
Tobacco juice and spit.
"When Toby has to hold his spit fer a long time, the ambeer runs out of both sides of his mouth an' looks plumb nasty."

Overheard . . .
"The hill was so steep you'd skin your nose a-climbin' it."

AMOUNGST
Among.
"Marvin was the onliest one amoungst them fellers that had on belt britches. All the rest of um had on duckins."

AMOUNT TO SOMETHIN'
Become successful.
"That Harrison boy is a-peddlin' Cloverine Salve, garden seeds, an' the *Grit* paper, all at the same time. Looks like he's gonna amount to somethin' some of these days."

AND ALL
And everything.
"With my crops done burnt up and all, looks like I ain't goin' to make nothin' this year."

AND THEM
And others, and the rest.
"We're goin' to see Mamma and them at Christmas."

ANGRY
Inflamed or red, said of a sore or a wound.
"You better doctor that foot 'cause it looks mighty angry to me."

ANTIGOGLIN, ANTIGODLIN
Leaning, not parallel.
>"That old barn's been antigoglin like that ever since I can remember, an' it ain't fell yet."

ANY SIGN OF
Any indication of.
>"See any sign of whir them shoats rooted out?"

ANYTHANG
Anything.
>"When a feller's family's goin' hungry an' he needs a job of work, he'll take jist anythang he can git."

ANYWAYS
Anyway, anyhow.
>"Taters is mighty fitten eatin' anyways a body is of a mind to fix um."

APERN
Apron.
>"They don't nobody never do no cookin' without puttin' on a apern."

A PIECE
A ways.
>"We live quite a piece from the mailbox, but it's on the way to school an' we don't have to make no extry trip 'cept when school's out."

A PIECE OF MY MIND
Verbally demonstrating one's pop-off valve.
>"Makes no nevermind to me that Wilma is double my size. I'm a-goin' over right now and give her a piece of my mind, and we might jist have us a tussle."

APPEARS TO ME
Seems to me.
>"Hit appears to me that women wouldn't want to git their hair bobbed off short like a man. An' when they use them hot curlin' arns it stinks like somebody's singein' chicken feathers."

ARGUFY
Argue.
"You put them two young-uns together an' all they'll do is argufy over the least little thang."

ARN
Iron.
"Mamma-she'd wash on Monday an' arn on Tuesday."

ARSH
Irish.
"Doyce jist has to have his Arsh taters an' beans ever day."

ASH HOPPER
A wooden hopper with a trough or spout for making lye by pouring water through hickory ashes.
"I druther make soap from lye out of a ash hopper anytime than that old store-bought stuff."

AS HIGH AS
As many as.
"I've seen as high as ten bales of cotton picked off of that patch."

AS HOW
1. That.
"Looks like hits a-comin' up a cloud so I reckin as how I'd better git a-gittin' on home."
2. Whether.
"I don't know as how I can make it till crops come in, without borrowin'."

A SIGHT OF
A lot of.
"I ain't never seen sich a sight of chiggers as that Doyle had on him when he got done blackberry pickin'."

ASKEERED
Frightened, afraid.
"Amos is askeered of bein' out after dark, skeered of boogers."

ASPERN
Aspirin.

"When I've got a sick headache a aspern don't do me no good. I pour me a BC powder on my tongue an' wash it down with a Co Cola. That's the onliest thang that'll knock it out."

AST
Ask or asked.

"Ain't no need to ast, 'cause I done ast Mamma an' she said we couldn't go."

A-TALL
At all.

"Guy don't thank nothin' of Mabel a-tall; she ain't nothin' but a slave to him."

Overheard . . .
"The dinner bell is always in tune."

ATHIST
Atheist.

"A athist is somebody that thanks they ain't no Almighty."

ATTER
After.

"Thank I'll mosey over around that old rail fence atter a while an' see if I can find me a mess of poke sallet."

AT THE DROP OF A HAT
At the slightest provocation.

"Ernie has got a mighty short fuse. He'll jump on you at the drop of a hat."

AUDERED
Ordered.

"I never knowed Mamma had done it till it come in the mail, but she'd set down an' audered me a airviator helmet out of the Monkey Ward catalog jist like Lindbergh's."

AUGHT
Naught, zero.
"If you ain't got nothin' to start with, an' you don't add nothin' to it, you still won't have nothin', 'cause aught an' aught is still aught."

AW
1. An expression of mild sympathy.
"Aw, I hope you git to feelin' better by tomorrow."
2. An expression of disgust.
"Aw, that old sow's done rooted out again."

A WAY OFF
Far away.
"Clyde jist up an' moved a way off sommers—Nevader, I thank."

A-WINDIN'
Tumbling.
"You've got to leave the spark lever up when you crank a Model T or it'll knock you a-windin'."

AX
Ask.
"I thank I'll ax her to go to the pitcher show with me Saturday night."

BABYIN'
Overprotecting, coddling.
"It's time you quit babyin' Edgar. He ain't never goin' to make it on his own if you don't."

BACK
1. To address a letter.
"I've done wrote the letter; now I have to back it an' stamp it."
2. Before the present.
"It was about two days back when I seen him."

BACK AND TO
To and from.
"I went barefooted back and to church, but I put my slippers on jist 'fore I got there."

BACKARDS AND FORWARDS
Forward and back.
"Shovin' that cross-cut saw backards and forwards from sun to sun's got me tuckered out."

BACK-DOOR TROTS
Diarrhea.
"They ain't nothin' that'll git away with a feller worser than gittin' a bad case of the back-door trots whenever he's tryin' to do a little courtin'."

Overheard . . .
"Pete is jist the kind of feller that was born tard an' raised lazy."

BACK STICK
A large log placed in the very back of the fireplace.
"That big old hickory back stick orta last all night."

BACK TALK
An impudent, insolent, or argumentative reply.
"I kain't stand a young-un that'll back talk."

BAD MAN
The devil.

"Ever young-un knowed what the Bad Man looked like—his pitcher was on ever can of Red Devil Lye. He was red all over an' had a pointed tail like a arrow an' toted a pitchfork."

BAD MOUTH
Criticize severely and persistently.

"He don't do nothin' else when he comes 'round but bad mouth ever'body."

BAD OFF
Very sick.

"Wilma Lou has been mighty bad off fer quite a spell. Hit wouldn't surprise me none if Jim Ed went fer the doctor jist any day now."

BAD PLACE
Grown folks and preachers call it hell but children aren't allowed to say that; they have to call it the bad place.

"Grandma says if Vernon don't quit tellin' all them stories he'll go to the bad place."

BAD TO
Inclined toward.

"This-here mule is bad to run away."

BAIL
1. The handle of a bucket or pot.

"Better git you a rag 'fore grabbin' that bail on that kittle 'cause it's hot enough to might near take the hide off."

2. Bell.

"When the farr bail rung, them volunteer farrmen was all ready to go in three minutes."

BAINTY
Bantam, a miniature chicken.

"A little bainty rooster can outcrow, an' a lot of times outfight, a full-grown one."

BAIT
1. More than a sufficient amount.
"I kain't hardly wait till them biddies git to be fryin' size. I got me a cravin' fer a bait of fried chicken."
2. Fill of.
"Whenever election time rolls around I'm goin' to vote aginst the whole bunch of them politicians that's in, 'cause I've had me a bait of ever last one of um."

BALANCE
Rest, or part remaining.
"The preacher was baptizin' an' he jist got two of um dunked when it come up a cloud. After the storm he done the balance of um 'cept fer two that chickened out."

BALLIN' OUT
Verbal abuse.
"The teacher didn't whup Melvin but he shore got a big ballin' out."

BARD
Borrowed.
"Horace run up a bunch of gamblin' debts an' got in so deep he even bard on his pickup."

BARK A SQUIRREL
Killing a squirrel by striking the bark on the side of the tree limb on which he sits, killing it by concussion.
"Wayne hardly ever put a mark on a squirrel whenever he went a-huntin'. He'd jist bark um nearly ever time."

BARKIN' UP THE WRONG TREE
1. Hunting dogs barking up a tree from which the hunted animal has fled (usually to another tree).
"Bruno never knowed that that-there squirrel's done swung acrost half a dozen treetops from the one he clumb up, so he's still barkin' up the wrong tree."
2. Being mislead or misplacing blame.
"Them that figgers Hoyt done it is barkin' up the wrong tree."

BARN DOOR'S OPEN
An unzipped or unbuttoned fly.
"Old man Barksdale's barn door's open nearly all the time. Reckin he ain't worried about nothin' a-pokin' out."

BATCHIN'
Living without the benefit of a woman in the house.
"Me an' Jim Ed's both been workin' on that project an' batchin'."

BATHLESS BATHROOMS

There wasn't no sitch a thang as a bathroom. The closest thang to it was a outhouse, er privy, if you want to talk fancy, but nobody didn't never take no bath in it. If a body was a-thankin' a-tall he'd build it downwind of the house 'cause after it gits a little age on it, it gits perty ripe, an' when the weather gits hot it's hard to git your mind off of it, 'specially at dinner time. Nearly ever time they'd be one-holers 'cause it's jist not the time when a body enjoys havin' company much. Lots of the tenant farmers didn't even have no outhouse, jist had to go to the barn er out in the woods.

Last year's Sears and Rareback's catalog was the wipin' paper, 'cept fer the slick colored pages. When it run out folks'd generally use corncobs er leaves. At night a chamber pot was slid under the bed er a slop jar was set over in the corner but a lot of the young-uns peed the bed and didn't wake up to use them nohow.

The ever'day personal cleanup was scrubbin' faces, necks, an' ears with a soapy washrag in the mornin' an' washin' feet in the washpan before goin' to bed at night. On Saturday the No. 2 washtub was brought into the house, water was warmed on the cookin' stove in a arn teakittle, an' the cleanest one got the first bath in the clean water. The last one in still wasn't very clean.

BAY-ED
Bed.
> "The doctor's had Betty Sue in bay-ed fer over a week, but she says it ain't done her much good."

BEAT ALL
Surpass everything.
> "Don't it jist beat all how folks can change? Ever since Willodean come into that money, her nose is so high it'd rain in it."

BEAT HIS TIME
Took his girl.
> "Tom don't go with Betty no more 'cause Jack's done beat his time."

BEAT'NEST or BEATINGEST
Something that surpasses all.
> "Hit's the beat'nest thang I ever heered tell of . . . that Ruzievelt a-gittin' 'lected fer the fourth time."

BEAT OF
That which or who surpasses something or somebody else.
> "I have never seen the beat of Miz Boyer. Even with them five head of young-uns too little to help much, she can raise an' put up more stuff than anybody I've ever seen."

BEAT YOU UP
Get up earlier.
> "I allus beat you up ever mornin'."

BEDBUG
Chinch.
> "I jist kain't stand to have no bedbug a-gnawin' on me. I'm gonna saturate ever crook an' cranny of them bedsteads an' sprangs with coal oil first thang Saturday mornin' an' try to git rid of them dadburn thangs."

BEDCLOTHES
Sheets, blankets, quilts, and the like.
> "That makes three sets of company that's slept on them bedclothes, an' I reckin I better wash um 'fore any more shows up."

BEDSTID
Bedstead.
"That-there old arn bedstid is the one that Mamma started keepin' house with an' it b'longed to her grandma, an' she had bought it second handed way back yonder."

BEE GUM
Bee hive.
"Use to, folks would make a bee gum out of a big old holler section of a black gum tree."

BEHOLDEN
Obligated.
"I ain't got no wife, don't owe a copper, live by my lonesome, an' ain't beholden to no livin' soul."

BEIN' AS
Since, because.
"Bein' as you got more than you can use, I reckin I'll take some . . . if you're shore you won't disfurnish yourself."

BELLYWASH
Carbonated soft drink, soda pop.
"I do love a great big old bottle of strawberry bellywash whenever I'm hot an' thirsty."

BETWEEN A ROCK AND A HARD PLACE
A dilemma, a situation involving a choice between equally unsatisfactory alternatives.
"Luvenia's sort of between a rock and a hard place. Her man treats her like dirt, but she kain't leave him 'cause she ain't trained to do no job."

Overheard . . .
". . . snow flakes as big as goose feathers."

BIDDIES
Baby chickens.
"That old Dominecker hatched off thirteen biddies out of fifteen aigs."

BIG
Famous, important.
"She wound up gittin' married to some big lawyer way out in Arizona."

BIG CHURCH
No church at all.
"The onliest church Luther b'longs to is the big church."

BIG DOIN'S

Use to, ever Fourth they'd be some mighty big doin's. There was all kinds of diff'runt contests an' games, like sack races, reg'ler foot races, baseball, horseshoes, climb a greasy pole, ketch a greasy pig, an' stuff like that.

They sold ice-cold lemonade an' reg'ler cold dranks like Nehi an' Co-Cola. They'd be buried in a big washtub full of ice. They all cost a nickel. Fer eatin', they was goat stew that cost fifteen cents fer a meat tray full with two slices of light bread.

BIGGEST TIME, BEST TIME
Much fun, enjoyment.
"We'd go to a box supper an' you'd eat what you brought, with the boy that bid highest fer it, an' then we'd daince an' have the biggest time."

BIGGETY
Self-important.
"Aw, he's so biggety they ain't nobody can stand him. I'd like to buy him fer what he's worth an' sell him fer what he thanks he's worth."

BIG MEETIN'
Religious revival.
"We been goin' to the big meetin' fer three nights right hand runnin'."

BIG MONEY
A great deal of money.
"They's big money in makin' shine but I'm jist skeered to fool with it."

BIG TO-DO
1. Stressing more importance than necessary.
"Ever'body made sitch a big to-do about the new preacher. It ain't his preachin', so it must be his looks."
2. Notable occasion.
"Ever fourth Sunday in May they have a big to-do at the Primitive Baptist Church in Sanderson."

BILED
Boiled.
"Them aigs was biled so long the yeller had got plumb powdery."

BITTER AS GALL
Extremely bitter, as bitter as bile.
"That medicine was as bitter as gall but hit done me a right smart bit of good."

BITTER WEEDS
A low-growing weed with a yellow flower that, when eaten by a cow, causes the milk to taste bitter.
"I reckin them shoats is a-goin' to be mighty glad we kain't drank no milk on account of the cow pasture bein' plumb full of bitter weeds."

BLACK STRAP
A very strong black molasses.
"Grandpa can allus eat a bate of that old black strap molasses, but I jist kain't stand the stuff."

B'LEEVE
Believe.
"I b'leeve in everlastin' life an' it's up to ever'body to decide whir they want to go: up Yonder er jist hope fer a back seat in hell."

B'LEEVE YOU ME
Believe me.
"I told Horace I wasn't about to marry him ner no other man. I got bad stung wunct and, b'leeve you me, it ain't gonna happen agin."

B'LONG
1. Belong.
"The VFW, American Legion, Lions, Elks, Masons, Rotary, Methodist church, an' PTA is jist some of what I b'long to, an' the old lady fusses at me most of what little time I'm home. I stay perty busy."
2. Deserve, should.
"You b'long to be whirever your man's at."

BLESS GOD
A mild oath.
"Bless God if I ever git done with this quilt I don't thank I'll never do another'n."

BLESS OUT
Tell off.
"When she gits stirred up enough she'd bless out a preacher."

BLINKY
Starting to sour.
"Set this-here milk back 'cause it's done got blinky."

BLOSSOMED OUT
Said of a girl who is making or has made the transition between a child and a woman.
"That little Sue Ann of Clarence an' Gertrude Ridgeway's that used to be so homely has done blossomed out an' made a real fine lookin' girl."

BLOW
1. Boast.
"He likes to blow about the thangs he's done but I bet he ain't done half of um."
2. Pant, gasp, breathe hard.
"I've got to let my horse blow 'cause he's about give out."

Overheard . . .
". . . too lazy to hit a lick at a snake."

BLOW A FIST
A low whistle sound produced by blowing between the thumbs when both hands are cupped tightly together.
> "W.G. could wiggle his ears, blow a fist, and roll his eyelids up on a match stick jist like a winder shade."

BLOWED UP
Pregnant.
> "Reva got tard of hoein', pickin' cotton an' thangs, so she run off sommers an' wasn't heard from fer six months. When cold weather come on, here she was all blowed up an' lookin' like she hadn't changed clothes er had no bath the whole time."

BLOWWAY *see* DOGTROT

BLUE JOHN
Low butterfat or skim milk.
> "I wouldn't have no durn Holstein cow. Oh, they give a heap of milk, but it ain't no richer than blue john."

BOBBY-CUE
Barbecue.
> "About the only thang better'n a big steak er good old fried chicken is bobby-cue . . . specially a hog."

BOB WARR
Barbed wire.
> "Amos shore ain't much of a rifle shot. He couldn't even shoot through a bob warr fence without hittin' it."

BOOGER
1. Something scary, like the booger man, or just the opposite.
> "Ain't he a cute little booger?"

2. Dried nasal mucus.
> "If a feller don't blow his nose it'll make a booger."

BOOGERY
Scary.
> "A bunch of boys went way back in Salt Peter Cave but I never went fer. It was too boogery."

BORN AND RAISED
Born and reared.
> "I was born and raised in the South, never been North, an' ain't aimin' to be caught thar neither."

BORN DAYS
One's life.
> "Never in all my born days have I seen anythang like that."

BORRY
Borrow.
> "Mamma wants to know if she can borry this quart fruit jar full of coal oil till the peddlin' man comes Wednesday."

BOTTOM DROPPED OUT
1. To rain very heavily.
> "It was last Tuesday evenin' when it come up the ugliest cloud you ever seen, an' fer half a hour the bottom dropped out."

2. To fall drastically in the stock market.
> "Lots of folks was a-flyin' mighty high back in '29 till the bottom dropped out."

BOTTOMIN'
Replacing chair seats (bottoms) with cowhide or by weaving materials such as cane or hickory strips.
> "Larkin Hendricks was the best hand at bottomin' chers that I ever knowed."

BOUGHTEN
Bought, as opposed to homemade or home grown.
> "I tried some of that boughten light bread but it ain't nothin' like biscuits."

BOUND TO
Sure to.
> "Bobby Lee lays down 'fore he even takes the cork out of a bottle of shine, 'cause he's bound to drank all of it at wunct an' he don't want to be bothered with fallin' down."

BOX YOUR EARS
Slap one's face.
"Young-un, the next time I ketch you a-pullin' that cat's tail I'm gonna box your ears fer you."

BRAINS AND EGGS
A dish consisting of fried hog brains and eggs.
"I jist kain't wait till hog killin' time so I can fry me up some good old brains and eggs."

BRAND-SPANKIN' NEW
Brand new.
"The mail rider has done went an' bought him a brand-spankin' new car."

BRANG, BRUNG
1. Bring, brought.
"Come over here an' set on my lap an' tell me what Sandy Claws brung you."
2. Give birth to, bore.
"That big old Poland China sow's due to brang pigs about the first of next week."

BRAR
Brier.
"Elmer seen this-here little old green snake on a big blackberry brar, an' he caught it by the tail an' popped its head off, jist like poppin' a whup."

BREAK
Age or become weak as one grows older.
"I ain't seen Bessie fer goin' on five year, but I hear tell she's startin' to break awful bad."

BREAK HIM FROM SUCKIN' EGGS
A threat or a determined effort to stop someone from engaging in some activity; originally meant to stop a dog from eating eggs from hen's nests.
"If I ever hear that he so much as looks at another woman, I'll break him from suckin' eggs."

BREAKIN' OFF
Clearing skies.
> "It's done quit rainin' an' it's breakin' off over yonder to the southeast."

BREAK UP HOUSEKEEPIN'
A divorce or separation.
> "I never knowed why Ben an' Lucy decided to break up housekeepin', but they shore done it an' she went back to her folks."

BRESH
Brush.
> "Mary Lou don't have to bresh her teeth no more 'cause she married a feller that wears a mustache."

BRICKLY
Brittle.
> "I use to jist love that hard peanut candy but it's so brickly I kain't chew it with my old sorry teeth no more."

BRILLIANTINE
Brand name of a thin fragrant liquid, red in color, used on the hair before combing.
> "Since I started puttin' Brilliantine on my hair I done quit Vaseline 'cause it's too greasy and it don't smell as good neither."

BRITCHES
Breaches, pants.
> "Ever one of them boys tore their britches goin' through that bob warr fence around my watermelon patch whenever I farred my shotgun into the air."

BROGAN SHOES
A coarse work shoe reaching above the ankle.
> "Them new brogan shoes is rubbin' the hide off of my big toe."

BROOM CORN
A tall cultivated stiff-branched plant used in the making of brooms and brushes.
> "I'm tard of havin' to pay them high prices fer brooms. I'm a-plantin' me a little patch of broom corn so I can make um fer myself."

BROUGHT ON
Boughten, store-bought.
"I ain't never wore nothin' 'cept fertilizer an' flour sack dresses. Ain't never had one that was brought on in my whole life."

BRUSH ARBOR
A quickly improvised shelter consisting of poles attached to trees, forming a framework over which brush is piled to make a roof, usually built as a temporary place of worship.
"We never had no church buildin' fer five year. Never had no money, so we had our meetin's in a brush arbor."

BUB
Bulb.
"Gertrude's so helpless she has to wait till her man comes home to change a light bub."

BUM
Bomb.
"Hit's some mighty scarin' times. Why, somebody could jist send over a bum in the middle of the night an' maybe blow up a whole county."

BUMFUZZLED
Bewildered, confused, unable to find an answer.
"How a body can git talkin' an' music right out of the air an' have it come through that-there radio has got me plumb bumfuzzled."

BURNIN' POWDER
Shooting a gun, usually implying missing whatever is shot at.
"A body that shoots a automatic gun is jist burnin' powder nearly ever time."

BURN UP
1. To cheat.
"I'm here to tell you she evermore burnt you up on that deal."
2. To make one very angry.
"Don't it jist burn up a body the way that Warshin'ton bunch treats a farmer?"

BUILDIN' A HOME WITH HAND TOOLS

Them that was well off, an' had a little dirt with a house on it, had whatever nice thangs that was a-goin' at that time. The balance of um done with mighty little. Tenant houses wasn't painted ner nothin', an' they was made out of logs er planks. They jist had walls on the outside an' the inside was jist the back side of the logs er planks. If there was timber on the place, that's whir the logs er lumber'd come from.

A two-man crosscut saw, a double-bit axe, a maul, an' wedges got the trees down an' cut up. Poplar trees made about the best logs an' lumber there was a-goin'. Folks'd take an' skin the bark off with a drawin' knife. It had a real sharp blade a foot long er more, had a handle on each end a-pointin' the same way the blade was, an' a feller pulled it torge him to git the bark skint off. If the logs wasn't no more'n a foot through, they was jist cut to length, notched, an' laid up. Now some of them poplars was two foot through er more an' needed flat'nin' an' smoothin' with a adz. A adz looks a little like a hoe but the short handle's got a curve in it, an' so's the blade, so it's angled jist right against the log. That blade's about sharp as a razor. A grindin' stone's allus handy fer keepin' it thataway.

A house's foundation is made out of rock pillers, an' any diggin', levelin', er smoothin' that's needed is generally done with a mattick. That's sort of like a hoe an' a pick mixed together. Shingles fer the roof are split out of a red oak with a froe. That's a tool that ain't sharp a-tall. You'll sometimes hear folks say somethin's as "dull as a froe." It sorta looks like a straight razor that's open an' ready fer shavin'. A maul, made out of about a foot and a half length of a six-inch saplin' is what you hit the top of the froe with to get the shingle started.

Even a log house has to have some sawmill boards fer the floor, doors, and sitch, an' them's the onliest thangs that ain't made with hand tools. Except fer a hammer an' nails, them's all the tools a body needs to build a log house.

BUTT IN
Enter a conversation uninvited, meddle or interfere with other people's affairs.
"Some young-uns ain't got no raisin'. Why, some of um will jist butt in whenever grown folks is talkin' jist like they ain't got no manners a-tall."

Overheard . . .
"Since Ed took sick, he's so weak he couldn't pull a settin' hen off of the nest."

BUTTON THE DOOR
To turn the door button to a horizontal position so it will hold the door shut.
"I better git up an' button the door so a booger won't jist walk in on us."

BY THE NAME OF
Named.
"A feller by the name of Stokes that lives down on Sheep's Ferry Road peddles them Watkins Products. He's got the best liniment an' black pepper they ever was."

BY THE SKIN OF HIS TEETH
A narrow escape, a near miss.
"He come back alive from that war but was jist by the skin of his teeth that he done it. He nearly got killed twict."

◄ C ►

CAG
Keg.
"Uncle Bud use to do barberin' on Saturday out under a big old oak by the side of the main road. He had him a set of Sears and Rareback barber tools, an' his barber cher was jist a nail cag."

CALABOOSE
A local jail.
"Ain't no tellin' how many times Charlie's been throwed in the calaboose fer gittin' drunk an' fightin'."

CALF SLOBBERS
Meringue.
"Jane's lemon pie allus has about two inches of calf slobbers on top."

CALL
Occasion, cause, need, excuse.
"Jim ain't got no call to treat Darlene an' them young-uns so bad."

CALL FOR CALF ROPE
To give up or admit you've had enough.
"This time I ain't gonna let you up till you call for calf rope loud enough for ever'body to hear you say it."

Overheard . . .
". . . aigs so big it only took four to make a dozen."

CAMRY
Camera, Kodak.
"Lori Mae, honey, run an' git the camry while the whole bunch of us is here so we can have our pitcher struck."

CANDLE FLY
Moth.
"That dratted candle fly jist went down the lamp chimley. That'll break him from suckin' eggs."

CANKER

1. An erosive or spreading sore.

"He's got the worst lookin' canker on his arm you ever seen."

2. A green or bluish deposit especially of copper carbonates formed on copper, brass, or bronze surfaces.

"Her neck is plumb green whir that 'gold' necklace has done cankered."

CAP'UM

Captain; sometimes used as a substitute for mister.

"Much oblige, Cap'um, fer lettin' me borry your tar pump."

CARRIED AWAY

Aroused to a high and often excessive degree of emotion or enthusiasm.

"I ain't never seen a body git so carried away about square daincin' as Dora Mae."

CARRY

Tote, transport.

"Pore old Misseries Rawlins ain't got no way to go, so I carry her to town wunct a week to git her groceries."

CARRYIN' ON

To behave foolishly or immorally.

"The way ever'body was carryin' on was a plumb disgrace."

CASIN'S

Automobile tires.

"I reckin hit's a perty good old flivver but the casin's is plumb slick."

CATAWAMPUS

Crosswise.

"He laid off them garden furs jist catawampus to what they ort to of been."

CAT-HEADS

Type of biscuit.

"Fer cat-heads, you make up your dough in a big loaf. You don't roll it out, you jist grab a hunk of it an' choke off a piece an' pat it out with your hands instead of rollin' it an' cuttin' it out with a biscuit cutter."

CHAINCE or CHAINCT
1. Risk.
"I wouldn't chaince gittin' tied up with Ruby—she's one more pistol."
2. Opportunity.
"If Marshall ever gits a chainct to make somethin' out of hisself he'll amount to somethin'."

CHER
Chair.
"Come on in an' have a cher. Had your dinner?"

CHEW THE RAG or CHEW THE FAT
Talk.
"Y'all come by right after church an' we'll have time to chew the rag a spell 'fore we eat dinner."

CHILE
Child.
"A chile kain't be no chile but wunct an' folks shouldn't orta try to push um to be like grown folks so quick."

CHILLERN
Children.
"Ethel has had a head er two of chillern ever year since her an' Lawton has been married."

CHIMLEY or CHIMBLEY
Chimney.
"Folks that ain't got no farrplace chimley has to leave the door unlocked so Sandy Claws can git in."

CHIST
Chest, as a cedar chest, hope chest, or a chest of drawers.
"Willodean's hope chist is slam full, but now that she's 42 an' looks like she's been whupped with a ugly stick, there jist ain't much hope left."

Overheard . . .
"Betty ain't zackly ugly, but she looks a heap better at a distance."

CHITLINS or CHITTERLINGS
The small intestines of pigs cooked and eaten as food.
"Folks that ain't never eat none call um chitterlings; the ones that have know they're chitlins."

CHIVAREE or CHARIVARI
A noisy mock serenade to newlyweds.
"I reckin them idiots never heard that a chivaree wasn't 'spose to last all night."

CHUNK
Throw.
"If my dog ever comes over to your place, jist chunk a rock at him!"

CHURN RAG
A rag loosely wrapped around the dasher handle to keep milk from splashing through the hole in the churn's lid.
"Somebody take that churn rag an' wipe that young-un's nose. You know how I 'spise nastiness."

CIVIL
Polite, courteous, kind.
"I never seen sitch a ill-mannered bunch in my life. They wasn't even civil to nobody."

CLABBER
Sour milk that has thickened or curdled.
"Lots of folks thank they're too high brow to drank clabber, but they'll turn right around an' put out big money fer the same thang with the water squeezed out of it, called cottage cheese."

CLARE
Clear.
"Woodrow is a mighty close man. He'll keep bilin' the same old coffee grounds till he ain't got much more'n clare water fer drankin'."

CLEAN
Completely.
"Viola is as mad as a wet hen at Clivas 'cause he clean forgot to git her some snuff when he was in town . . . an' she had it wrote down, too."

CLEAN HIS PLOW
An aggressive action.
"If he ever lays a hand on one of my young-uns, I'll clean his plow fer him."

Overheard . . .
"They call her 'Radio Station'; anybody can pick her up, especially at night."

CLUMB
Climbed.
"Jerry clumb up to the top limb of that big old sweet gum an' punched that coon out amoungst all them dogs."

COAL OF FIRE
A piece of glowing charred wood, ember.
"Mamma sent me over here to borry a coal of fire 'cause our fire went out an' we ain't got no matches."

COAL OIL
Kerosene.
"Blow out that light out yonder in the kitchen if they ain't nobody usin' it, 'cause the peddlin' wagon's chargin' 8 cents fer coal oil now."

COAM
Cone.
"They ain't nothin' no better'n a big old coam of strawberry ice cream."

COBBLED UP
To make or put together hastily.
"You ain't never seen sich a cobbled up mess as that shack that them Jacksons has to live in."

COGITATE
To think or study about something.
"I'll jist have to cogitate a while about askin' Miz Judy to marry me. We'll both look at thangs diff'runt ten year from now."

COLD-COCK
To knock one unconscious.
"If a feller ever done me the way he done you, I'd jist cold-cock him."

COME IN ON
To visit someone unexpectedly.
"We didn't hardly know them McIntosh folks—was jist neighbors fer about a month one time—an' they come in on us last month with four head of young-uns an' stayed fer a week."

COME OUT
Pay out of debt.
"With all the dry weather we've had, I don't know if my crops is gonna make good enough fer me to come out at gatherin' time."

COMIN' ALONG
Growing up.
"When I was comin' along, young-uns never had much time to do no playin' 'cause there was allus some work to be done."

COMIN' DAY
Daybreak.
"It's comin' day an' we've got to be in the field by sunup to git a full day's pay."

COMIN' UP A CLOUD
Expression to indicate an impending storm.
"It's comin' up a cloud an' it looks mighty boogery. We'd better head fer the barn."

COMMENCED
Began, started.
"That preacher opened up the Good Book an' commenced to preach right at me, it looked like."

CONNIPTION FIT
A fit of rage.
"Lee throwed a conniption fit whenever Bonnie Mae run his good handsaw into a nail."

CONSUMPTION
Tuberculosis.
"Mr. Gladney wasn't nothin' but skin an' bones when consumption finally took him to his final reward. They burnt the mattress an' other beddin', scalded the sprangs an' slats, an' sunned the bedstid fer days."

CONTRARY
Disagreeable, stubborn.
"I don't know which one of um is the most contrary, my old woman or my mule."

COON'S AGE
A long time.
"I don't know whir old John got off to. I ain't seen him in a coon's age."

COOTER
Turtle.
"There ain't no better eatin' than a good cooter whenever hit's fixed right."

CORK
Caulk.
"I'm goin' over yonder to Mr. Melin's an' see if I can borry his corkin' gun so I can cork around that winder whir that cold air is whistlin' in."

CORN DODGER
A small, usually round, baked or fried corn cake.
"All them folks had to eat fer supper was mustard greens an' corn dodgers."

CORN PONE
Corn bread made without milk or eggs.
"Some corn pone and turnip greens pot likker, along with a big glass of buttermilk is mighty fitten eatin'."

CORN SHUCKIN'
Removing the husk from an ear of corn.
"We used to go to a corn shuckin' an' ever'body'd come an' work their fool heads off. When we got done we allus had some big doin's like a square daince."

COTTON
Take a liking to, approve of, catch on.
> "I jist don't cotton to these newfangled ways like talkin' on a wire an' flyin' around in the air like a bird."

COUNTERPIN
Counterpane, bedspread.
> "All of Misseries Callahan's counterpins had the pertiest embroidery on um that a body ever seen."

COUPLIN' POLE
A long pole, as on a wagon, which couples the front and rear axles; holes bored in the pole through which a coupling pin may be dropped adjust the wagon's wheelbase.
> "We use to take time about ridin' the couplin' pole. Ever'body liked it best."

COWED DOWN
Depressed with fear.
> "It's pitiful the way Harland's got them young-uns so cowed down—his old lady, too. They kain't even look at you over a second at a time."

COW PIE
Cow feces, meadow muffin.
> "Watch out that you don't cut your foot on that big fresh cow pie."

COW'S TAIL
Last.
> "It don't matter what we're doin' er whir we're goin', Marvin's allus the cow's tail."

CRACK
To leave slightly open.
> "I'm burnin' up in here with that big farr in the heater. Crack that door a little an' put the arn in front of it so it won't blow shet."

CRACKLIN' BREAD
Corn bread made with cracklin's (pieces of fried pork skin) in it.
> "It's been quite a spell since I've had me any good old cracklin' bread, but it's hard to git the cracklin's to make it."

CRACK OF DAY
Daybreak.
"We're gonna pull out in the mornin' at the crack of day."

CRAWFISH
Back out of a deal or situation.
"A handshake jist ain't good enough no more. It has to be in writin' er a lot of times folks will crawfish."

CRAWL HIS FRAME
Attack him.
"It was a good thang that Tonnis finally shet his mouth about Dorene, 'cause Virgil was a-gittin' ready to crawl his frame."

CRAZY AS A BESSIE BUG
Extremely crazy, out of one's mind.
"You must thank I'm as crazy as a bessie bug fer ridin' in that flyin' machine an' you might jist be right."

CRICK
A stiffness.
"Lum has to hold his head sideways like that 'cause he's got a bad crick in his neck."

CROPS ARE RUNNIN' AWAY
Grass and weed infested.
"My crops is runnin' away. The Johnson grass an' crap grass has jist about got too fer ahead of me."

CROSS WORD
Abusive language.
"Ruby an' J.P. still act like they're newly-weds. I don't reckin there's ever been a cross word between um."

CURIOUS
Eccentric.
"Old lady Perkins is really a good old soul; she's jist curious."

CUSSIN'

Cursing is an integral part of regional slang, and old-timey Southerners called it cussin'. As one old timer was known to predict: "Cussin' rots teeth."

The more fiery versions aren't fit to print, but substitutions for the real thing added emphasis and humor to everyday speech. Even children were sometimes allowed to use such cuss words as dad-burn, dad-gum, dad-blame, dang, darn, durn, doggone, drat, heck, or shucks.

Mild cussin' utilized such phrases as "shoot farr" or "Lordy, Lordy," or "Law me." "Lordy, mercy" means "Lord have mercy" literally, but its usage did not, generally, have any religious meaning.

CUT A RUSTY
Show joy, show off, dance vigorously.
"Mance Elrod use to really cut a rusty at square dainces doin' that double-shuffle of his."

CUT IN
Enter an ongoing conversation without being invited.
"Ain't hardly nothin' more ill-mannered than fer a young-un to cut in when grown folks is a-talkin'."

CUT OUT FOR
Suited or trained for.
"Wayford jist ain't cut out for no store clerk job."

CUT THE FOOL
Act in a comic or foolish manner.
"One is about the same bad as the other'n. Ever time whenever Floyd er J.C. gits together they both allus like to cut the fool."

CUTTIN' UP
Behave in a comic, boisterous, or unruly manner.
"Ray is allus cuttin' up in class; that's why he gits a "D" in deportment."

DAB
A small amount.
"Maybe I can git a job an' make a dab of money to hold me till fall."

DADDY
To beget a child.
"All that low-down man of Virginia's has ever done fer her was to daddy all them young-uns."

DAINCE
Dance.
"I daince a spell an' git to sweatin' an' then I start to stinkin' an' then nobody won't daince with me no more."

DAINCIN' AROUND LIKE A CHICKEN ON A HOT STOVE
Energetic, hurried movements.
"Looked like Melvin's feet hardly touched the floor—he'd be daincin' around like a chicken on a hot stove."

DANGERSOME
Risky, dangerous.
"Goin' up in one of them flyin' contraptions is mighty dangersome."

DARK-THIRTY
About a half-hour after darkness comes.
"The school bus broke down an' them young-uns never got home till about dark-thirty."

DARKEN THE DOOR
Literally, to stand in the doorway thereby cutting off much of the light, but figuratively, to visit a home when unwelcome.
"Because of the way you done my little girl, drankin' er no, I'm givin' you fair warnin' to not never darken the door of my house agin."

DAWG
Dog.
"I hear tell they's folks a-livin' in town that keeps dawgs right in the house with um. I jist couldn't live that nasty myself."

DAYDOWN
The pink of the evening, just after sundown.
"The pertiest part of the day jist has to be right at daydown."

DAYUM
Damn.
"Dayum, it's cold. I never got this cold even when I was a-workin' up in Detroit City."

DEAD AS A DOOR NAIL
So dead there would be absolutely no chance of recovery.
"That little boy of Clyde's shot that big old chicken hawk with a .22 an' killed it dead as a door nail."

DEAD AS A HAMMER
Really dead.
"Them flashlight batteries is as dead as a hammer, been dead so long they've spewed out a lot of that old acid an' prob'ly rurnt my good flashlight."

DEAD ON ONE'S FEET
Extremely tired, worn out.
"Tired as Jim was, he finally made it till quittin' time, but he was dead on his feet."

DEAD TO THE WORLD
Unconscious, asleep, drunk, in a faint.
"It didn't take over five minutes after Ed's head hit the piller till he was dead to the world."

DEEF
Deaf.
"He was deef in one ear an' couldn't hear out of the other'n."

DEEP ENOUGH TO DROWN A HUNDERD-YEAR-OLD MAN
Much deeper water than would be required to drown a young man.
"Bobby Lee thought he could wade across the creek, but about ten feet out he stepped in a big hole deep enough to drown a hunderd-year-old man."

DEPITY
Deputy.
> "A depity is a feller hard by the High Sheriff hisself an' he's got jist as much power to take people in."

DEPORTMENT
Behavior, conduct.
> "Ray use to have to stay in a lot at recess er after school, an' he allus got a bad grade in deportment."

DESPISABLE
Unworthy of consideration or interest.
> "There ain't a more despisable old woman in the county than Miz Roberts and her young-uns too."

DEVIL
Tease, banter.
> "Old Ben loves to devil folks but he don't mean no harm."

DEVIL'S HORSE
Praying mantis.
> "They's two thangs I'm deathly skeered of, that's a snake an' a old devil's horse; a snake'll likely kill a body an' a devil's horse can put out a eye if he spits in it."

DEW POISON
Dew, believed to be poisonous to wounds on the foot.
> "If you've got a cut on your toe durin' dog days you better walk on your heel early in the mornin' while the dew's on, so you don't git dew poison in it."

DIFF'RUNT
Different.
> "Wiley Snodgrass takes an' puts his overalls on backards jist to be diff'runt."

DINNER
The noon meal in the South.
> "I cut wood fer old man Turner an' he give me fifty cents a day an' dinner."

DIPPIN' SNUFF

Pulverized tobacco, or snuff, was frequently "dipped." The "dipper" usually places the snuff between the teeth and lower lip, sometimes on the side. Older snuff-using women didn't usually dip it. Instead, they used sweet gum toothbrushes. A green gum twig two or three inches long and about half the size of a pencil was selected. The bark was then removed. One end was chewed on until it became a soft brush. The moistened brush could then be dipped into a box of snuff and a small glob would cling to the brush. The whole thing (except for the unchewed end) was placed between the teeth and cheek. Teeth could be brushed (if there were any) using the snuff as a polish.

DIRECTLY
Soon, after a while.

"I heered the thang but couldn't pick it out. Then directly I seen it. Shore-nuff hit was a airplane!"

DIRT
Land.

"Bein' a hard hand or sharecroppin' is all Dayton's ever done. He ain't never owned a foot of dirt hisself."

DISFURNISH
Deprive, be in short supply.

"Well, bein' as your aigs is about to rurn an' you kain't git shed of um . . . an' yore right shore you won't disfurnish yourself, I reckin I could take a dozen of um off of your hands."

DISREMEMBER
Forget or forgot.

"Saw a feller t'other day that said he knowed you. Maybe he said he was kin, but I disremember his name."

DIVIDE
Share.
"Don't y'all be hoggish with them goobers. Divide with the little-uns."

DOB
Apply a substance to a surface with a finger, cloth, or brush.
"I'll take an' dob a little dab of this Cloverine salve on that sore, an' that ort to fix it up in no time."

DOES FOR
Helps.
"You won't find no finer feller than Morris Gallion. He allus does for old folks an' widders an' won't never take nothin' fer it."

DOCTORS AND MIDWIVES

A body'd have to be mighty bad off to send fer the doctor. But if you needed one bad enough to call on him, he'd jump in his buggy an' come on out whir he figgered on gittin' paid er no. There wasn't hardly any cash money an' a heap of times he might git a ham, chickens, er a sack of taters fer payment, er a promise of cash in the fall when crops come in, but back then it was more important for doctors to treat folks than to git rich.

Some folks spent their whole life without never seein' no doctor. Even when they got borned a granny woman brung um into the world. Them midwives done more ketchin' babies than doctors back then anyhow. Fer some thangs you had to call in somebody that had a special "gift" fer curin' certain thangs. Curin' the thrash (thrush) in babies is one of the thangs I'm talkin' about. Different ones use different kinds of doctorin'. One is to have a stranger to give the baby a drank of sprang water out of his hat. Another'n is fer the person with the gift to blow in the baby's mouth three times, no more, no less. The third one is to pass the baby backwards through a white mule's collar.

Overheard . . .

"The chimley drawed so good it'd suck a body's hat right off of his head."

DOGGED IF I KNOW
An expression meaning I don't know or I don't remember.
"He made out like he knowed somethin' about doctorin' horses. He could uv been as good as he talked but dogged if I know."

DOG IRONS
Andirons, support for logs in a fireplace.
"Dog irons that stand up too high in front make it mighty hard to git a back stick in."

DOG TIRED
Very tired.
"Whenever I come in dog tired, I want me a woman that'll have plenty of good hot vittles fixed fer me."

DOGTROT, BLOWWAY
A roofed passage, similar to a breezeway, which connects two parts of a cabin.
"They was two big log rooms with a dogtrot between them."

DOMINECKER
Dominicker or Dominique, a Plymouth Rock chicken.
"You can tell when a feller's dumb about chickens when he don't know a Barred Rock from a Dominecker."

DONE
Already.
"I've done finished my studyin'."

DONE-DONE
Already finished.
"I'm done-done with this-here knife an' I licked it clean, if you want to use it now."

DONE WITH
Finished.
> "My gatherin' is done with now, so I reckin I can jist start on cuttin' my winter farr wood."

DOODAD
A small article whose common name is unknown or forgotten.
> "I use to have a little doodad fer fixin' that, but I don't know whir it got off to."

DOODLY-SQUAT, DIDDLY-SQUAT
Nothing.
> "Homer blowed all his money on gamblin' an' now he ain't got doodly-squat."

DOOHICKEY
Doodad.
> "Buster whittled a little doohickey out of a stick that was handy fer helpin' to git your shoes on."

DOOJIGGER
A gadget.
> "I need me some kind of doojigger to put my cookin' spoon on."

DO ONE OUT OF
Cheat.
> "Tommy is the kind of feller that'd do his grandma out of her old-age pension if he had a chainct."

DOPE
A popular carbonated cola believed to contain dope.
> "Give me a Dope, a pack of peanuts, an' a Moon Pie. I love to pour them peanuts in my Dope, jist a few at the time, an' a Dope is mighty good fer takin' headache powders with too."

DOST
Dose.
> "I druther take a dost of medicine er take a whuppin' than to hit that cotton field in the mornin'."

DO WHAT?
Used in asking a person to repeat what he said.
"Do what? I hope you never said what I thought you said."

DOUBLE SUBJECTS

Old timers were often heard to use two subjects to refer to the same person or object. The two nearly became one in speech. Some examples:

"Bill-he rurnt his brand new britches on that bob-warr fence."

"Mamma-she never had no time to rest."

"Them-there teachers, they was strict."

"That-there snake-hit was all quiled up."

DOWN
Unable to get around because of sickness, bedfast.
"Mr. McBride's folks has all been down with the flu fer over a week"

DOWN IN THE MOUTH
Sad, depressed.
"Gil is down in the mouth 'cause he couldn't git home fer Christmas."

DOWN ROW
The row of corn that is mashed down by the wagon at gathering time.
"If a feller gathers corn off of the down row all day he kain't hardly straighten up his back when he gits done. Hit's worser'n pickin' cotton."

DOWN TO A GNAT'S HAIR or EYEBROW
Very precise.
"Larry-he thanks ever'thang ort to be done down to a gnat's hair. He shore-nuff does do mighty perty work."

DRAM DRANKER
A social drinker, one who drinks in small quantities.
"Tom shore wasn't no dram dranker; he'd turn up a pint fruit jar of shine an' not take a breath till he saw the dry bottom."

DRAW UP
Shrink.
> "Better git a size bigger'n you need, 'cause soon as they're washed they'll draw up."

DREAN
Drain.
> "A busted radiator's somethin' I shore don't need, so I'm gonna drean it till this cold spell's over with."

DRINK AFTER
To drink from a previously used and unwashed vessel.
> "Levonia won't drank after nobody but she uses the water bucket dipper to pour water in a glass, an' it's done been drunk out of lots of times, on both sides."

DROP
Give birth to a child or animal.
> "That old cow's got to drop a calf 'fore long er she's gonna bust."

DROP OFF
Go to sleep.
> "Soon as I git done eatin' my supper I'm allus about ready to drop off."

DROPPED HIS CANDY
Did wrong or made a mistake.
> "Hobert shore dropped his candy when he let a fine woman like Miss Kate get away from him."

DROVE WELL
A water well driven or drilled with machinery as opposed to a hand-dug well.
> "If a feller has to go way down deep to hit water, it'll have to be a drove well."

DROWNDED
Drowned.
> "Billy Joe drownded that litter of kittens. He put um in a tow sack with a rock an' chucked them in the creek."

DRUMMER
A traveling salesman.
"I git most of my goods fer the store from a drummer out of Nashful."

DRUNK
Drank.
"I drunk a whole pint of shine an' I laid down before I drunk it so I wouldn't have to bother with fallin' down."

DRUTHER
Would rather.
"I druther hoe cotton than to pick it any time."

DRUTHERS
Choice.
"If I had my druthers I'd allus plow with a mule instead of a horse."

DRY GOODS
Textiles, ready-to-wear clothing, and notions as distinguished from hardware and groceries.
"Old man Morgan made all his money with two dry goods stores and paddin' the books."

DUCKINS
Overalls.
"Most folks call duckins *overalls*, but some of the folks from the North say *bib overalls* instead of jist sayin' *overalls* er *duckins*. It don't make no sense, though, 'cause ever'body knows that all overalls has got bibs."

DUDS
Clothing, personal belongings.
"I tried fer ten year to live with that man. Finally I jist couldn't take him runnin' over me no more, so I tuck my duds an' left."

DUMPY
Short and fat.
"Them Farnsworth young-uns is all dumpy, but they're pretty as a speckled pup under a red wagon."

◄ E ►

EARLY DON'T LAST LONG
An expression meaning time flies.
"'Fore the dew gits off I've got to pizen them tater plants an' then hoe out them beans. I'll do good to git done by dinner 'cause early don't last long."

EAT
Ate.
"I done eat but that pie shore looks good."

EAT A BITE
Eat something.
"Why don't y'all jist stay an' eat a bite with us? We got plenty."

ELBOW GREASE
Hard work, extra effort.
"Some folks is pretty good cotton pickers an' some extry good. A feller by the name of Wilton Eubanks could pick as high as 300 pounds a day—that takes a heap of elbow grease."

EPIZOOTICS
A disease that is hard to describe or put a specific name to.
"Opal had a real bad case of the epizootics, they said, an' dang near died."

E'RE ONE
Either one.
"I'll jist make you a present of e're one of them-there puppies you want."

ER
Or.
"Pete's an' Gladys' young-uns is allus ketchin' somethin' er done caught somethin' er is gittin' hurt."

ET
Eaten.
"Come on in an' take dinner with us if you ain't done et."

EVENIN'
Afternoon; night begins at six o'clock.
"Jim and Bertha invited their new neighbors from up North to come over for homemade ice cream yesterday evenin', but they never showed up till seven o'clock at night."

EVER
Every.
"Percy is the best horseshoe pitcher of the bunch. He can pitch a ringer near bout ever time."

EVER'THANG
Everything.
"Denver-he went to one of them carnivals an' played them gamblin' games an' they tuck him fer ever'thang he had."

EXCUSIN'
Except, not counting.
"Robert the janitor told me, 'I got nine head of young-uns, excusin' one that died last night.'"

EXTRY
Extra.
"Elvin, you done a extry good job of bottomin' that straight cher fer me so I'm givin' you a extry quarter."

◄ **F** ►

FAIRED OFF
Skies cleared.
"Hit stopped rainin' an' faired off 'fore dinner."

FAIR TO MIDDLIN'
Pretty good.
"How you been gittin' along, John?"
"Oh, fair to middlin', I reckin."

FALLIN' OFF
Loosing weight.
"Sue Ellen has kind of been under the weather an' you can tell she's fallin' off too."

FALLIN' OUT
Disagreement, not on speaking terms.
"I ain't seen ner one of um since they had that fallin' out."

FALL OUT
Become exhausted.
"I got so hot workin' out thar in that garden in the middle of the day that I thought fer a while I was goin' to fall out."

FALSE FACE
Mask.
"You couldn't tell one young-un from the other'n at Halloween, 'cause ever last one of um had on a false face."

FANGER
Finger.
"That little Johnson boy gits made fun of 'cause he's got a extry fanger on both of his hands."

Overheard . . .
"Somebody drunk J.W.'s whisky, and it made him mad as a snake."

FANNIN' THE COVERS
Raising quilts or blankets high enough to let cold air under.
"Mamma, make Ray quit fannin' the covers. He's doin' it on purpose an' I'm about to freeze."

FARD
Forehead.
"That young-un's actin' puny. Let me feel his fard; I thank he's runnin' a fever."

FARR
Fire.
"Young-uns that play in the farr of a evenin' will pee the bed, I've heered tell."

FARRBOARD
Fireboard, mantel.
"That Big Ben clock's been up on the farrboard fer over twenty year."

FARR WOOD
Larger pieces of wood burned in a fireplace or heater for warmth, as opposed to stove wood which is used in a cooking stove.
"When the crops are gathered there is a little restin' time 'fore startin' in on cuttin' winter farr wood."

FA-SO-LA SANGIN'

Short "Sangin' Schools" were held in the churches throughout the South to teach Christian harmony. The "Sangin' Master" used the shaped-note system made famous by Billy Walker. A triangle represents fa, an oval for so, a square for la, and a diamond for mi, and so on. Musical instruments were not generally used; a tuning fork set the pitch.

FATTENIN' HOG
A hog that is grown and fattened for the family's use.
"We allus put in a garden, had a milk cow, an' raised a fattenin' hog."

FAVORED
1. Looked like, resembled.
"Millinee favored her daddy but she is the onliest one that did. Them twins look like Silas Morgan, that used to be their hard hand, an' maybe fer good reason."
2. Was partial to, preferred.
"Tom's favored his left leg ever since that horse throwed him."
3. Gave in to, let someone have his or her way.
"Jim never would fuss with Irene, he jist favored her."

FELL DOWN IN HIS GRADES
Made lower than usual grades in school.
"Harry's report card is awful. He's done fell down in his grades twict."

FELLER
1. Fellow.
"I kain't stand a feller that won't say what he has to say to your face, instead of talkin' behind your back."
2. Boy friend.
"Gertie Mae's jist about grown . . . she's done got her a feller."

FELL OUT WITH
Not on speaking terms.
"Jerry fell out with Nadine last Saturday night an' it looks like the engagement is off."

FER
1. For.
"Feller said he'd take two bits fer it."
2. Far.
"We don't have fer to go—couldn't be more'n a mile."

FER PIECE
A long way.
"Mabel an' them lived a mighty fer piece from town."

FIGGER
Figure.
"I've heered folks say that them flyin' contraptions will be haulin' folks around in the air jist as common as cars an' busses."

FINE
Nice.
    "That shore was a mighty fine dress, fer a pore woman, that she had on."

FIRE STICK
Poker, generally of wood.
    "Save that old hoe handle, it'll make a mighty good fire stick."

FIRST LIGHT
Daybreak, dawn.
    "By first light we've done had breakfast of a mornin'."

FIT
Fought.
    "One time they was two fellers that liked the same gal an' neither'n was gonna put up with the other'n a-goin' with her. Well, one day they met up with each other on the road an' they stepped down out of their buggies, drawed their knives, an' fit each other till they both cut each other to death right on the spot."

FITH
Fifth.
    "That fith grade teacher must of been a Yankee. She was a-tryin' to make us b'leeve we lived in North America, an' I jist up an' told her that I didn't live in no North America, I lived in the South, South America."

FITTEN
Fit, suitable.
    "Don't b'leeve I've ever had more fitten grub than what Misseries Thomas fixes."

FIVE-AND-TEN-CENT STORE
A variety store that originally sold only 5-cent and 10-cent items.
    "Allus the biggest joy in goin' to town was seein' the stuff in Woolsworth five-and-ten-cent store and havin' a nickel or two to spend."

FIX HIS WAGON
Do something harmful or abusive to someone.
    "If I ever find out who stold my dog, I'll fix his wagon."

FIXIN'

1. Planning on.
"I'm fixin' to box some ears if you young-uns don't behave."

2. Preparing.
"Mamma's fixin' some polk sallet fer dinner."

FLAT

Unquestionably, without a doubt, plain.
"I jist flat told him to not never come around me no more whenever he's been a-boozin'."

FLESHEN UP

Take on weight, become fat.
"Doris is skinny as a dirt dobber. She'd look a heap better if she could fleshen up a little."

FLEW INTO

Attacked.
"That high-tempered fool jist flew into that feller with both fists fer little er nothin'."

FLITTER

Fritter, pancake.
"Harold tuck a big old rock an' mashed that snake's head flat as a flitter."

FLOP-EARED

Having the upper portion of the ear bend outward from the head.
"No wonder Alton is flop-eared. His hat is three sizes too big an' it sets right down on top of his ears."

FLOWERDY

A floral pattern.
"Audry don't have to wear no flour-sack dresses no more, I reckin. I seen her in a right perty flowerdy dress at the sangin'."

FLUX

Diarrhea.
"Somethin' tore up Nadine's stomach up an' give her a terrible case of the flux."

FLY OFF THE HANDLE
Get very angry.
"If you want to see somebody shore-nuff fly off the handle, jist bad mouth one of Bobby Lee's young-uns."

FLY PAPER or RIBBON
A special paper covered with a sticky substance which holds flies which light on it; paper is laid on flat surfaces and the ribbon hung from the ceiling.
"Next time we go to town I hope I have a few nickels left to buy some fly paper and fly ribbon. Them flies is as thick as bees around a hive."

FLY SPECKS
Housefly dung.
"I ain't about to eat this piece of pie that was left out of the safe. It's got fly specks all over the calf slobbers."

Overheard . . .
". . . too lazy to open a umbrella an' hit a-rainin'."

FOB
A short strap, ribbon, or chain for attaching to a pocket watch.
"Somebody give Floyd a pretty leather fob with a brass steam engine on the end of it."

FOEMAN
Foreman, the boss man.
"It give Carl a bad case of the big head when he got made a foeman."

FOLLER
Follow.
"Mr. Eubanks has got a hound that can foller a day-old coon track even if he was a-walkin' on Tom Walkers."

FOOL WITH
To spend time on something without any particular advantage or purpose.
"I jist pure love to fool with my flowers."

FOOT-FEED
Automobile accelerator pedal.
"Old-man Greer never did buy nothin' but Model Ts, 'cause he didn't take no stock in no foot-feed ner no shiftin' lever."

FOOT LOG
A log placed across a stream to form a foot bridge.
"When the creek rises an' gits swift an' muddy, I kain't walk no foot log, 'cause it makes my head swim."

FORED
Forward.
"Ain't no tellin' how many times a body goes backards an' fored plowin' a ten-acre field."

FORTY 'LEVEN
A great number.
"I bet I heered that yarn forty 'leven times but I still git tickled at it."

FORTY WAYS FROM SUNDAY
In all directions simultaneously.
"It's a good thang there wasn't no third place in that boxin' match. Joe Louis knocked that feller forty ways from Sunday."

FOUND
Gave birth to.
"My old sow found six fine pigs last Wednesday, four of um gilts."

FREE FER NOTHIN' or FREE GRATIS
At no cost.
"Misseries Walker said that when Queenie finds her pups I can have one of um, free fer nothin'."

FRENCH HARP
Harmonica.
"Nat was allus a-blowin' an' suckin' on a french harp, an' got to whir he could make one of them thangs talk."

FROLIC
Party, romp.
"It's mighty rough on a feller puttin' in a day's work after spendin' all night at a frolic."

FROM CAN TO KAIN'T
From the time one is able to see until one can't, daylight till dark.
"If you thank sun to sun is a long day, try workin' from can to kain't."

FRONT ROOM
Living or visiting room.
"I shore wish I had me a nice Chesterfield sofa fer my front room. We ain't got nothin' but straight chers to set company on."

FUR
Furrow.
"Larkin ain't got no planter so he has to drop his corn in the fur by hand an' cover it up with a hoe."

FURER
Further, farther.
"From whir we live hit's a heap furer to the mailbox than it is to the store."

Overheard . . .
"Ox Wingate was big enough to go bear huntin' with a switch."

◄ G ►

GABBIN'
Talking.

"I tried to do a little gabbin' with that new feller that opened up the eyeglasses place, but I couldn't 'cause we couldn't understand each other. Folks say he come from Massytoosets."

GALLINIPPER
A very large mosquito.

"An old-timer said that maybe the reason they call them a gallinipper is that they jist keep on suckin' till they get their gallon."

GALLOWSES
Suspenders.

"He allus stuck his thumbs in his gallowses, rared back, an' throwed out his belly whenever he was tellin' off a big yarn."

GAME
Hurt, crippled.

"Herbert Watson ain't likely to ever forgit football playin', 'cause that game leg of hisn jist might last him fer life."

GAPPIN'
Yawning.

"Gappin' must be ketchin'. Now you got me doin' it."

GARNTEED
Guaranteed.

"This-here's a genuine 17-jewel Elgin watch an' chain, garnteed to last a body ten years."

GATHERIN' TIME
Harvest time.

"I'll shore be glad when gatherin' time gits here, 'cause I'm tard of not havin' no money to jingle."

GAWK
Stare stupidly.

Whenever Henry gits to town he has to gawk at ever girl he sees."

GEE or YEA
A command to a work animal to turn to the right.
"That old mule ain't never learnt gee. He don't know nothin' but haw 'cause he's allus been hooked to a turnin' plow and never has to turn to the right."

GET A STRIPIN'
Get a whipping with a switch, severe enough to show marks.
"Gittin' a whuppin' is one thang, but gittin' a stripin' makes a feller look like a red an' white zebra."

GET CAUGHT
To become pregnant unintentionally.
"Mavis use to brag that she knowed all about what she was doin' an' wasn't about to get caught. Well, I wonder what Miss Know-It-All has to say now about havin' to stand sideways to reach the door handle?"

GETTING DOWN TO THE SHORT ROWS

This expression meaning "nearly finished" came from the practice of terracing crops on sloping terrain. Rows paralleled the terraces but the terraces were not parallel to each other, so there were small triangle-shaped pieces between the long rows that were left over. Short rows were planted in these small areas and they were always the last ones to be cultivated or harvested. When one got down to the short rows, he was almost finished with that field.

GILLION or ZILLION
A very large number.
"If I've told you wunct, I've told you a gillion times not to exaggerate."

GIT A-GITTIN'
Get going.
"I reckin we better git a-gittin' so we can make it home an' milk an' feed the stock 'fore night."

GIT AWAY WITH
Embarrass.
> "I ain't never had nothin' to git away with me as much as when I slipped an' fell in the branch an' had to crawl out with my clothes a-stickin' to me, in front of ever'body."

GIT DONE
Finish.
> "I can't never git done with one thang till it's time to start on another'n."

GIT DOWN
Become disabled.
> "I better go see me a punchin' doctor about my back er I'm liable to git down with it."

GIT EVEN WITH
To cause another a social or business loss through spite.
> "It's a whole heap easier to forgive somebody if you git even with um first."

GIT HIS GOAT
To annoy or irritate someone.
> "George has got a weak belly so if you want to git his goat, jist start talkin' about him a-eatin' dead chicken fer dinner."

GITTIN' HITCHED UP
Getting married.
> "After havin' good sense fer thirty-six years Pete's finally lost his mind an' is gittin' hitched up."

GIVE
Gave.
> "Mr. Tom Watson give me the biggest old watermelon you ever seen."

GIVE OUT
1. Announce, state.
> "They never give out the names of the ones that done it, but I reckin ever'body knows anyhow."

2. Become exhausted, fail.
> "If I don't have me a big breakfast, I'll give out 'fore dinner."

GIVE UP TO BE
Acknowledged to be, accepted as.
"He's give up to be the best fire-an'-brimstone preacher that ever hit this part of the country."

GIVE YOU OUT
Decided you weren't coming.
"That feller from the city told Clivas he'd be there 'fore dinner an' he never showed up till nearly five o'clock. They told him, 'We waited on eatin' dinner till two o'clock, an' by that time we'd done give you out.'"

GOAT
A lustful (generally old) man.
"That old goat thanks the women are crazy about him, but the truth is they kain't hardly stand him."

GO IN A-WASHIN'
To go swimming in a lake or stream and take a bath while at it.
"Aubry ain't about to take no reg'ler bath but he will go in a-washin' in the summertime."

GO IN WITH
Share the cost.
"I'd like to put in about two acres of tobacker but I ain't got the money to buy the seed an' fertilizer. You want to go in with me on the halves?"

GOIN' WITH
Dating.
"Bess has been goin' with that sorry old boy fer months. I shore hope she don't end up a-marryin' that sapsucker. She'd jist be rurnt."

Overheard . . .
"I don't chew my tobacker twict." (What I say I say only once.)

GOOBERS
Peanuts.
"It don't make no nevermind if they're raw, biled, er parched, I do love goobers."

GOOD HAND
1. Skilled.
"Uncle Bud was allus a mighty good hand at killin' hogs an' cuttin' up meat."
2. Good, dependable worker.
"Mr. Lewis shore got him a good hand whenever he hard Willis Norton."

GOOD LONG WHILE
A long time.
"It's been a good long while since it's been cold enough to see your breath."

GOOD MANY
Several, lots.
"They's a good many folks that tell me them yeller maters is a heap better'n red ones. They look like to me they'd taste like a cantaloupe."

GOOD NEWS BEE
A bee about the size and color of a yellow jacket which looks and hovers motionless like a tassel fly; its "stinger" part is flattened rather than rounded and there is no stinger.
"They say when the good news bee hovers near you, it is bringing good luck and if it should light on you, that's very good luck."

GOOD SIZED
Big.
"Them's a good sized pair of mules. I bet they could pull a 19-inch plow all day an' never have to blow."

GOOD STAND
A row or field of plants with satisfactory spacing due to a high percentage of germination.
"I didn't git no good stand of corn in that field. I reckin I'll jist have to replant."

GOOD WAYS OFF
Far away.
"I hear there's a lot of cotton pickin' in Arkansas, but that's a good ways off fer a feller that would have to hobo to git thar."

GOOSE-DROWNDER AND FROG-STRANGLER
A very, very hard rain.
"We was over on the fer side of the creek when it come a goose-drownder and frog-strangler. Wellser, that creek got so high we couldn't git back across till way up in the mornin' the next day."

GOOSE-EGGED
Zero score.
"Ever time I play horseshoes with old eagle-eye Pete Wilson, I git goose-egged."

GOOSEY
Ticklish.
"Some folks say if you hold your breath you won't be so goosey."

GOOZLE
Throat, Adam's apple.
"Looks like his big old goozle runs plumb to the top an' bottom of his neck ever time he takes a swaller."

GOPHER
A burrowing land tortoise.
"If it hadn't been fer gophers back in hard times we wouldn't uv had no meat at all."

GOT HIS EARS LOWERED
Got a haircut.
"Since Melvin got his ears lowered he looks plumb quare. Whir all that hair was it's nearly white as cotton an' down below it's as red as pokeberry juice."

GOT NO USE FER
Do not like, hold in low esteem.
"She's jist as two-faced as twin snakes, an' I ain't got no use fer her."

GOT OFF OF
Obtained from.
"This-here twenty-two is the one I got off of Darwin Ezell—traded him a coon dog fer it."

GOT ON THE GOOD SIDE
Became friends with or gained special favors.
"Hit pays to git on the good side of your gal's mamma an' daddy while you're gittin' on hern."

Overheard . . .
"I love her better'n a hog loves slop."

GOT TO GO OUTDOORS
The equivalent of "got to go to the bathroom," if there had been one.
"When you've got to go outdoors real bad, it's a terrible feelin'. One time I had to go outdoors so bad till I couldn't make it to the bushes an' had to drop my britches whir folks could see me."

GO TO MILL
Take a turn of corn to the grist mill to be ground into meal.
"Saturday I've got to go to mill and git coal oil the same trip. Hope I don't spill none on my meal er it will rurn it."

GO TO THE BAD
Spoil.
"Take this bucket of milk down to the sprang. I don't want it to go to the bad a-settin' in this hot kitchen."

GOUGE
Poke.
"If I drop off durin' the sermon, jist gouge me in the ribs."

GO WRONG
Stray from the straight and narrow.
"Hit's a big job raisin' a family, the way thangs is today, 'cause young-uns can go wrong so easy."

GRABBLE or GRAPPLE FOR FISH
To use one's hands to search in underwater rock crevices for fish.
"Some folks jist pile off into the creek an' grabble fer fish, stickin' their hands way back in them holes in the rocks, but you won't ketch me a-doin' no sich a thang. I'll pick me another way to be stupid."

GRANNY WOMAN
Midwife.
> "A heap of folks thank *midwife* is a little more uptown talk, but it's still a granny woman in my neck of the woods."

GRAVEYARD DEAD
Dead beyond a shadow of doubt.
> "If I ketch that possum in my henhouse, he'll be graveyard dead."

Overheard . . .
"Brother Maxie's mouth opens an' shets jist like a prayerbook, but it's fer from bein' wun."

GREEN AS A GOURD
Untrained, inexperienced.
> "Ain't no need of puttin' Albert on that job, he's green as a gourd an' wouldn't be of no more use than tits on a boar hog."

GREE-UTS
The way some Southerners pronounce *grits*, especially ladies.
> "If a body is a little short on hen aigs, all you got to do is throw a spoonful of gree-uts on the plate with one aig an' it'll be like eatin' two."

GRINDIN' STONE
A large circular sharpening stone that is either turned by hand or is foot powered.
> "If a feller has a set of pedals on his grindin' stone he don't need nobody to turn it fer him."

GRINNIN' LIKE A HORSE EATIN' BRIERS
A very broad grin.
> "When I looked across the table an' saw Marlene grinnin' like a horse eatin' briers, I knowed who had got my pully bone."

GRINNIN' LIKE A POSSUM
As above.
> "I ain't never seen a young-un as proud as Marsha whenever she won the spellin' bee. She was grinnin' like a possum."

GROWIN' FOOD

If folks was goin' to eat durin' hard times in the rural South they'd better raise it er grow it, 'cause money was scarce as hen's teeth. Soon as sprang come ever'body started breakin' up their gardens an' gittin' ready to plaint um. Horse an' cow hockey was used fer fertilizer. It was the best an' it was free.

Even before the garden started comin' in you could go along old fence rows an' find nice new tender shoots of poke sallet. Maybe it was jist 'cause folks was hungry fer somethin' green, but it seemed to be jist as good as turnip, mustard, er collard greens. Radishes an' green onions'd come in first. Chop um up fine an' pour hot bacon grease over um makes a mighty good wilted salad.

Boiled new potatoes along with English peas made a mighty good combination. The best kind of green beans was Kentucky Wonder pole beans, an' a few pods of okry cooked on top was mighty fine. You could plaint the beans in the corn row an' not have to stick um. The best corn was the field kind an' white was better'n yeller.

Folks killed hogs when it got cold enough to see your breath an' the sign was right. Hams, shoulders, an' lean bacon could be smoked to make it keep, an' sow belly could be salted down but a lot of the fresh meat like liver an' lights had to be eat right off the bat er it'd rurn. Next mornin' after hog killin', a larrupin' good dish was brains an' hen eggs with a few pieces of sow belly fried real crisp.

GULLY-WASHER
A very heavy rain.
"Looks like we're a-gonna git a gully-washer 'fore dark."

GUMPTION
Common sense, initiative.
"A body'd thank if a feller went plumb through school he'd have a little gumption, but Clyde did an' he still don't know his nose from a hole in the ground."

GUY
Tease or make fun of.

"You better not never guy Wilton about nothin'. If you do, it makes him mad as farr, an' he might knock you a-windin'."

Overheard . . .
"Don't hit a hornet's nest with a short stick." (Don't take unnecessary chances.)

◄ H ►

HACK
Embarrass, tease.
"It'd allus hack Irene whenever menfolks'd come by unexpectedly an' she'd have her underthings like teddies, bloomers, an' stuff out on the clothesline."

HAD IT IN FOR
Disliked or hated.
"Doug didn't never have no chance at them good jobs 'cause his fo'man had it in for him."

HADN'T OF
Hadn't.
"If Malcolm hadn't of joined the CCC, his folks woulda jist been up aginst it."

HAIL
Hell.
"If a feller is stupid enough to go down to that county-line jook joint, it's a good place to git the hail beat out of him."

Overheard . . .
"Joe Don looks like he's been a-sortin' wildcats." (Said of someone who's been bruised, cut, or scratched, or maybe all three.)

HAINT
Ghost.
"Ever'body says that old Walker place is hainted, but I ain't never seen a haint thar ner nowhere."

HANKERIN'
A strong or persistent desire.
"Ever wunct in a while I git a hankerin' to bum around an' hobo a while."

HAR
Harrow.
"After a feller turns his land he generally takes an' runs a spike-toothed har over it to break up the clods an' smooth it out 'fore plantin'."

HARD HAND
One employed at manual labor or general tasks.
"Mr. Sandlin sent his hard hand with a team of mules to pull us out of the mud hole."

HARDHEARTED
Unfeeling, pitiless.
"He's so hardhearted he'd shoot a doe deer layin' down with twin fawns a-suckin' on Mother's Day."

HARD LOOK
Look of disapproval.
"When I tuck that last biscuit off of the plate Mamma shore did give me a hard look."

HARD ROAD
Paved highway.
"Ronnie an' Marie live way back yonder so fer in the woods they have to pipe in daylight. It's four miles off of the hard road."

HARD ROW TO HOE
A difficult task.
"Old man Mashburn kain't hardly git out of the yard an' the onliest young-un that's big enough to work run off an' got married. Misseries Mashburn has got a hard row to hoe tryin' to do fer all them little fellers jist a-takin' in washin'."

Overheard . . .
". . . fried chicken so good it'll make you slap yore grandma."

HARD TIMES
Times of deprivation, having only the most basic necessities.
"It was mighty hard times in them Hoover days."

HARRISON & RICHERSON
Mispronunciation of Harrington & Richardson, firearms manufacturer.

"Stan swapped Mylan out of his nice Harrison & Richerson pistol, and now he ain't even got nothin' to shoot snakes with."

HATEFUL
Full of hate, deserving of or arousing hate.

"They ain't nobody that can stand that woman; she's the most hateful thang I ever seen."

HAVE YOUR PITCHER STRUCK or MADE
Have your picture taken.

"They had a machine whir you could drop a quarter in it an' have your pitcher struck."

HAW
A command to a work animal which means to turn to the left.

"That travelin' salesman didn't know gee from haw. Matter of fact, he hadn't even seen a mule before."

HAWG
Hog.

"She ain't no Poland China ner no Duroc ner nothin' special, jist hawg."

HEAD AND EARS
Completely submerged.

"I was baptized right thar in that-there creek, an' I mean head and ears, in that cold water."

HEAD FULL OF SENSE
Intelligent, smart.

"Lamar's so shy an' quiet that folks might not realize it, but he's got a head full of sense."

HEAD OF CHILDREN
A term used to denote the number of children.

They ain't no tellin' how many head of children that Misseries Perkin's got. They run all the way from married young-uns to courtin' young-uns to field young-uns to yard young-uns to floor young-uns to lap young-uns an' another'n er two that's a-waitin' on gittin' born.

HEAD SWIM
To be dizzy.
"I kain't go on them rides at the fair 'cause they make my head swim."

HEAP
Many.
"A heap of folks don't like buttermilk, but I'll take it over sweet milk any day."

HEAP SIGHT
Much, a lot.
"The other feller's job an' his wife both look a heap sight better'n they really are."

HEARD TELL OF
Heard of.
"I've heard tell of a two-headed calf, but I ain't never seen one myself."

HEERED
Heard.
"I heered we're liable to git a Republican in the White House this time, an' if we do, the farmer is rurnt."

HELLO
Used instead of knocking on the door.
"I hello-ed four er five times 'fore I roused anybody."

HELT UP
1. Robbed.
"The robber that helt up Archie never got nothin' but a Barlow knife, a Ingersol watch, an' a few coppers."
2. Endured.
"Misseries Washburn lost both of her boys in the war an' her man died the same year. How she helt up to it all without bein' sent to the bug house is more'n I'll ever know."

HEN APPLE or FRUIT
Hen egg.
"Some folks started callin' a hen egg a hen apple er hen fruit, jist to act smart er show out, I reckin."

HEN SCRATCHES
Poor penmanship.
"How in the world a druggist ever makes out them doctor's hen scratches is more'n I'll ever know."

HEP
Help.
"I shore do need me a job bad. You know of anybody that needs any hep?"

HERN
Hers.
"I reckin Eunice had ever right to buy material fer them two dresses, 'cause that egg money was hern anyhow."

HESH
Hush.
"Y'all young-uns jist ain't stayin' out till after nine o'clock on a week night, an' you might jist as well jist hesh your mouth about it."

Overheard . . .
"Larkin's new hard hand's like a blister—he don't show up till after the work is done."

HET
Heated.
"We het the house on eight cords of wood last winter."

HEY
Hi.
"Hey. All of y'all gittin' along all right?"

HIDE
Skin.
"When Jesse fell down on that graveled road, he skint the hide off of his arms, elbows, an' knees but didn't git a scratch on his face. Must uv had his head up like a fence lizard."

HIDE NER HAIR OF
No trace of.
"I ain't seen hide ner hair of my razor strop. I wonder whir it got off to."

HIGH AS A CAT'S BACK
Very high priced.
"I ain't goin' to trade at Barnett's Store no more, 'cause his stuff is high as a cat's back."

HIGH ON THE HOG
Living well beyond the ordinary.
"If folks knows how to git on that givement handout they can live high on the hog."

HIGH POCKETS
Nickname for a tall person.
"The one that made the most goals fer the team was allus High Pockets."

HIGH SHERIFF
Elected or appointed sheriff, not a deputy.
"Folks liked Leroy Blankenship so good that they kep on 'lectin' him fer high sheriff till he got too old to run."

HIGH TEMPERED
Capable of becoming extremely angry.
"Willard is likely to fly off the handle about any little thang. He's as high tempered as a rattlesnake."

HIGH TIME
About time.
"Hit's high time they put somebody up in Warshin'ton that's fer the pore man."

HIND CATCHER
A behind-the-plate baseball catcher.
"When Alvin plays hind catcher the pigtail gits a lot of practice runnin' down the balls he misses."

HIRED OUT
Worked for compensation.
"Whenever them young-uns hired out to somebody they never got to keep none of the money, had to give it all to their daddy."

HISN
His.
"Martin, you give that ball back to Harvey an' play with yourn. You know that one is hisn."

HISSELF
Himself.
"Mance lives all by hisself. Says he likes batchin' better'n bein' bossed around by some woman."

HISSIE FIT *see* CONNIPTION FIT

Overheard . . .
"Lonesomeness was a-settin' with me."

HIT
It.
"Hit is a lot more often that *hit* is used to start a sentence than to be in the middle of one, I thank."

HITCHED
Married.
"Old George went an' got hisself hitched to that high-tempered redheaded girl that had a young-un that wasn't hisn."

HITCH UP
To hitch one or more animals to a wagon, buggy, plow, or whatever is to be pulled.
"Ever time I try to hitch up that sorry old mule he tries to kick me."

HOBBLIN'
Walking with great difficulty.
"Old man Mashburn is still hobblin' along with his walkin' stick."

HOBO
A professional tramp, one who steals rides on freight trains; to live like a hobo.
"I knowed a hobo one time that had a pocketful of money and hoboed jist fer the fun of it."

Overheard . . .
"Marie's house was so nasty it would gag a maggot."

HOCKEY
Defecate.
"I druther take a hockey out in the woods than inside, like at the courthouse er depot. It jist seems nasty to hockey right in the house."

HOECAKE
A small cake made of cornmeal baked on top of the stove, formerly baked on the blade of a hoe.
"Ain't nothin' better'n a hoecake fer bread at supper time."

HOE HAND
Someone hired to cultivate plants with a hoe.
"Marie ain't much of a hoe hand but she can pick 300 pounds of cotton on her worst day."

HOGGISH
Greedy.
"Sometimes grown folks is so hoggish that when young-uns have to eat at the second table there ain't hardly nothin' good left."

HOG JOWL AND BLACK-EYED PEAS
A traditional dish eaten on New Year's Day for good luck.
"They ain't never been a New Year's day that I didn't have me a mess of hog jowl and black-eyed peas."

HOG'S HEAD CHEESE, HEADCHEESE, SOUSE
Foods using the edible parts of a hog's head, peppers, and spices.
"Hog killin' time is what I allus look forward to, 'cause I love hog's head cheese better'n a hog loves slop."

HOLD ONTO YOUR HAT
Be prepared for some shocking news.
> "If you thank what Coach Nugent done with that basketball player was a big stink, jist hold onto your hat."

HOLD OUT
Last, endure.
> "I'm so tard I don't know whir I'm gonna hold out till I git done."

HOLD YOU UP
Overcharge for goods or services.
> "I do all of my tradin' down at Shelton's 'cause they don't never hold you up fer their stuff."

HOLD YOUR HORSES
An expression meaning don't be in such a hurry, calm down.
> "Y'all jist hold your horses. Dinner ain't goin' to be ready fer a hour."

HOLLER
1. Yell.
> "If you need me fer anythang, you jist holler."

2. Hollow.
> "I seen a rabbit run into that old holler log over yonder."

3. Valley.
> "I live down in the holler by a creek."

HOLLER UNCLE
Give up, admit defeat.
> "When I git J.C. down I'm gonna hold him till I hear him holler uncle."

HOLP
Helped.
> "If the neighbors hadn't pitched in an' holp the old woman when I was down, I don't know what we'd uv done."

HOOVER GRAVY
A homemade gravy consisting of shortening, flour, and milk (if you had a cow; if you didn't, substituting water for milk).
> "Some folks will say cream gravy, flour gravy, white, er brown; I still call it what I allus have—Hoover gravy."

75

HOOVER HAM
Fatback.

"I've et so much Hoover ham that I'm use to it now an' I'd jist as soon have it fried right crisp as to have shore-nuff bacon er ham."

HORSE BLANKET
A large-sized bill (currency) in use before a switch to much smaller bills occurred in the late 1920s.

"A feller couldn't even git one of them horse blankets in the pocket books they make now."

HOME REMEDIES

Might near ever'body knowed somethin' about doctorin' with home remedies. In the wintertime the young-uns'd wear a cake of asifidity in a empty Bull Durham sack tied around their necks. That was to keep from a-gittin' colds, flu, an' stuff like that. It stunk so bad nobody'd git close enough to give you nothin' nohow. If you did git somethin' anyway though, there was lots of cures fer it.

Fer breakin' up coughs an' congestion a spoonful of sugar with a few drops of coal oil in it was hard to beat. Coal oil was good fer soakin' a hand er a foot in to draw out the pizen in a bad cut er somethin'. Holdin' chewed-up tobacker on a insect sting was good. Durin' the wintertime a body's blood gits thick an' sassafras tea in the sprang'll thin it out. Then a dose of calomel'll clean you out good on the inside.

Jist about ever'body'd keep these medicines on hand to keep from gittin' thangs an' to cure um if you did: Black Draft, Calotabs, calomel, caster oil, Epsom Salts, aspern, Castoria, Watkins er Sloan's Liniment, Nervine, Carter's Little Liver Pills, cod liver oil, Vicks VapoRub, Cloverine Salve, Vasoline, iodine, peroxide, Ludens Cough Drops, 666, Blue Jay Corn Plasters, alum, Lydia E. Pinkham, an' a bunch more.

HOMEY STUFF AND REG'LER DOINGS

Ever'body had a room fer company that most called the "front room" 'cause it was the frontest wun, even if there was jist two all put together. There wasn't no davenport fer settin' on, jist straight-back cane-bottom chers an' a rocker. The nicest thang in the room was a chifforobe er a chiffonnier er maybe the bedstead. Ever room 'cept the kitchen had beds in um. The bottom mattress was filled with straw er cornshucks an' the top one was a featherbed. There wasn't no reg'ler bedrooms. There wasn't nothin' on the floor 'cept sometimes a 9 x 12 piece of linoleum.

Some houses had a farrplace an' the other'ns had arn er tin heaters. Cookstoves was arn an' burnt wood. Skillets an' kittles was all arn too. By the back kitchen door, er out on the back porch if there was one, was the water bucket an' dipper, a washpan, hand towel, an' a lookin' glass. Wash water was jist throwed out in the yard; dishwater went into the slop bucket fer the hogs.

Coal oil lamps was used fer studyin' lessons an' eatin' supper an' breakfast by but they wasn't burnt much. Generally folks got to bed by 8:30 an' was up by 4:30. The winders an' doors didn't have no screens on um an' flies an' skeeters was perty bad. The only fans was a piece of pasteboard stapled to a wood stick that the funeral homes put advertisin' on an' give out fer free.

Most folks didn't take no paper 'cept maybe the Grit. When radios come out a few people that could git a hold of a little money got one of um but they had to be the battery kind an' wouldn't play long 'fore runnin' down. They mostly jist listened to the Grand Ole Opry on Saturday nights. Folks jist never knowed about much so they didn't never have much to worry about.

HORSEPITAL
Hospital.
"They tuck Sam to the horsepital in a ambulance with the siren a-goin'."

HOW COME?
Why?
"I'm allus jist a little bit late to git in on the good stuff but the first one to git in on the bad. How come?"

HUMDINGER
Someone or something remarkable.
"That new V-8 Ford of D.J.'s shore is a humdinger."

HUNKER
Squat.
"You got to hunker down behind a log er some bushes er them turkeys will spot you ever time."

HUNNERD
Hundred.
"Some say the school principal makes a hunnerd dollars a month but I doubt it. That's a awful lot of money."

HUSH
Shut up, be quiet.
"You young-uns jist hush when grown folks is talkin'."

HUSH PUPPY
A fried cornmeal fritter, originally used as food for dogs, now a popular bread for humans to eat with fish.
"I ain't eatin' no fish if I kain't have no hush puppies to go with them."

Overheard . . .
"It was a shore-nuff wilderness, ignorant of the axe."

I'D BE PROUD
An expression of pleasure or honor.
"Yes, I'd be proud to do fer Martha while she's down with the baby."

I DECLARE IN MY TIME or WELL, I DO DECLARE!
Expressions denoting surprise or amazement.
"I declare in my time, I ain't never seen as much damage as whir that toynader hit."

IDJUTS
Idiots.
"They's nine head of us young-uns an' they ain't ner one of us that turned out to be idjuts."

IDLE-MINDED
Not thinking.
"Oh, I'm so idle-minded I've done burnt my pie."

I DO KNOW
An expression of surprise or amazement.
"Well, I do know. I kain't b'leeve that little Judy is done a mamma."

I DOUBLE-DARE YOU or, stronger, I DOUBLE-DOG-DARE YOU
Dares, as powerful as they come.
"When a feller says, 'I double-dare you,' he's pretty mad; but when he says, 'I double-dog-dare you,' watch out—he's fightin' mad."

IDY
Idea.
"Emma Jean's all blowed up like a punkin, an' I got a idy it was that feller that drifted by here an' worked at Blanchard's gin durin' cotton pickin'. I seen her with him wunct a-comin' out of the bushes lookin' sort of flushed an' right smart tousled."

IFFEN
If.
"I'll be thar iffen the good Lord's willin' an' the creek don't rise."

IF IT'D BEEN A SNAKE IT WOULDA BIT ME
A statement used to express surprise that an item, thought to be lost, was really close at hand.
"I knowed I'd had my paper of pins a-pinnin' the dress pattern on my gingham jist a minute ago. I jist looked ever'whir an' finally found um right in my apern pocket—if it'd been a snake it woulda bit me."

ILL
Angry, vicious, bad-tempered.
"He's allus ill with his old woman an' them young-uns."

I'LL BE . . .
An expression of amazement, often followed by such phrases as "darned," "dogged," "a monkey's uncle," or "a suck-egg mule."
"I'll be a suck-egg mule. That little old wormy young-un turned out to be a big football player."

ILL-MANNERED
Sadly lacking in manners.
"Marvin, don't pick boogers out of your nose at the table; it's ill-mannered."

Overheard . . .
". . . too stingy to give you the time of day."

I'M HERE TO TELL YOU
An expression of agreement or emphasis.
"I'm here to tell you, I shore ain't goin' to eat no hog guts no matter what they call them."

IN A BAD WAY
Very ill.
"Tonnis is in a bad way since he fell out of the loft. He never broke nothin' but he got pretty well stove up anyhow."

IN A BIG WAY
Fun-loving, merry, frolicsome.
"No matter how bad thangs git, she's allus in a big way."

IN A FAMILY WAY
Pregnant.
"Ruby was already in a family way 'fore her an' Harry got married. You might say their 'I did's' came before their 'I do's'."

Overheard . . .
"Lonnie's so ugly his mother had to borrow a baby to take to church."

I NEVER DONE IT
An expression of innocence.
"Floyd said I was the one that broke out that winder light but I never done it. I throwed the ball to him an' he was the one that batted it."

IN HIS TIME
During one's prime, during one's lifetime.
"I've seen Mr. Ramsey outwork any three average men in his time."

INSTID
Instead.
"I druther peck hockey with the chickens instid of takin' somethin' that wasn't mine."

IN THE DEAD OF THE NIGHT
The middle of the night.
"Dan finally showed up, drunker'n a skunk, in the dead of the night."

IN THIS DAY AND TIME
Now, at this time.
"In this day and time, they's boys that's plumb sots 'fore they're sixteen year old."

I SWEAR IN MY TIME
A very mild oath.
"I swear in my time, I ain't never seen a woman run down as fast as Misseries Davis. A while back she was plumb plump an' now she's jist skin an' bones."

IT GOT TO WHIR
Regressed, deteriorated, worsened.
"It got to whir we jist couldn't git along so we broke up housekeepin'."

ITTY-BITTY
Little, teensy-weensy.
"Hit shore was a surprise to see Edna a full-grown woman. Last time I seen her she was jist a itty-bitty thang."

IT WAS A WHILE BACK
Some time ago.
"I 'member when thar wasn't but one house 'tween here an' town . . . but it was a while back."

Overheard . . .
"Julia's about as fat as a darnin' needle—she could stand under a clothesline in the rain an' never git wet."

JACK-LEG
Semiskilled.
> "He's jist a jack-leg carpenter, but if it's jist repair work Mike ort to handle it all right."

JACK-OF-ALL-TRADES
A person who can do passable work at various tasks.
> "Ernest can pick up a job of work jist about any time 'cause he's a perty good jack-of-all-trades."

JAW
Talk just to be talking.
> "I jist love to go to town on Saturday; they's allus a big bunch to jaw with."

JAY BIRD
Naked.
> "I never even knowed about bathin' suits, we allus jist went in jay bird."

JENNY BARN
Whorehouse.
> "When the jenny barn caught farr ever'body piled out in their underdrawers er birthday suits, even the mayor an' two preachers."

JIST
Just.
> "Jim Stafford said he was walking through the woods with a real pretty girl when she put her arm around his waist and said to him, 'I'm willin' fer you to do jist whatever you're of a mind to.' So he looked down at a big holler log and saw a big old frog, so he picked it up and shook it at her!"

JIST ABOUT
Almost.
> "I jist about had me a big buck deer but my danged old gun snapped on me."

JOB
Jab.
> A feller could jist job his fanger at Vernon, an' he was so goosey he'd near bout go wild."

JOB OF WORK
A job, usually of short duration.
> "I got me a two- or maybe three-day job of work next week helpin' to strang bob warr."

JOE-MULE
A male or horse mule (hybrid).
> "That little old joe-mule of mine ain't but fifteen hands, but he's the pullin'est little mule I ever seen."

JOOK or JUKE JOINT
A place to dance and drink with music provided by jukeboxes.
> "On Saturday night you'll allus find Alvin in some jook joint a-chug-a-luggin' beer."

JOY RIDIN'
Riding for the pleasure of it, with no predetermined route or destination.
> "First thang Thelbert does when he gits hold of a little money is to put a dollar's worth of gas in his Model A an' go joy ridin'."

JUBUS
Dubious, doubtful.
> "I'm allus jubus of a feller that don't look you in the eye whenever he's talkin' to you."

Overheard . . .
"More than two-thirds of the lies Wayford tells ain't true nohow."

◄ K ►

KAIN'T
Can't.

"I kain't never git as warm, seems like, by a heater as I can by a fireplace. I reckin seein' the farr is what makes the diff'runce."

KAIN'T CALL HIS NAME
Can't remember his name.

"Jake has got him a new sharecropper, but I kain't call his name."

KAIN'T HARDLY
Can, but just barely.

"I kain't hardly see thangs close no more, but a way off yonder I can still see perty fair."

KAIN'T-HELP-ITS
An ailment which impedes one's activities.

"If it wasn't fer my bad case of kain't-help-its, I'd be out thar on that floor a-daincin'."

KARN
Carrion, dead and decaying flesh.

"When a buzzard's been eatin' karn an' you git him skeered, he'll puke on you, they say."

KEEPIN' COMPANY
Courting, dating.

"I hear tell old Doc Newman's been keepin' company with the widder Perry fer the last month. You reckin there's anythang to it?"

KEER
Care.

"Donna said she wasn't gonna like me no more but I don't keer, 'cause I'll jist go an' git me another'n."

KEP
Kept.

"Tonnis jist kep right on pickin' on Bobby till he got tard of it an' picked up a stick an' knocked a goose egg on his head."

KETCH
Catch.
> "A rabbit's been in the garden; I seen his tracks this mornin'. I'm gonna bait up my rabbit trap an' ketch that sucker."

Overheard...
"... ugly as a mud fence after a rain."

KETCHIN'
Catching.
> "They say if a body's ever had the mumps they ain't ketchin' no more."

KETCH OUT
Catch and harness a mule or horse.
> "Dez was raised on concrete, right in Birmin'ham, an' didn't know what dirt was. He couldn't ketch out, hitch up, ner plough a fur."

KICKED ON
Complained.
> "You never kicked on the way I done 'fore we got married. Now you act like I ain't near good enough fer you an' your fancy friends."

KICKED THE TRACES
Threw caution to the wind.
> "Bert had him a good job an' a perty gal, but he got a bad case of ramblin' fever an' one day he jist up an' kicked the traces an' he ain't been seen ner heard from since."

KIN, KINFOLK
Relative(s).
> "When I went to the Miller Cemetery Decoration Day last year, folks was a-tellin' me that I was some kin (on one side er the other) to near bout ever'body that was buried there."

KINDLY
Kind of, somewhat.
> "It kindly gits my dander up when folks throw off on Otis fer his church beliefs. He may git to heaven 'fore they do."

KISS ON THE JAW
Kiss on the cheek.
"A kiss on the jaw like you git from kinfolks is all right, but it ain't nothin' like swappin' slobbers with your sweetheart."

KIT AND CABOODLE
The whole assortment.
"I bought the whole kit and caboodle fer $2.00 and a Barlow knife."

KITTLE
Kettle.
"I allus like to take the eye out of my stove an' set my arn kittle down in the hole whenever I cook my Kentucky Wonders."

KIVER
Cover.
"I near bout froze last night. I need a extry kiver er two on my bed tonight."

KNEE-HIGH TO A DUCK or GRASSHOPPER
Not very tall.
"I've knowed all them young-uns ever since they was knee-high to a duck."

Overheard . . .
"Ain't no tellin' how many folks he's beat out of their money."

KNOCKED IN THE HEAD
Foiled.
"The deal got knocked in the head 'cause I didn't have no credit."

KNOWED
Knew or known.
"They ain't no finer folks that ever set foot on this earth than them Luffmans. I knowed um fer years an' years 'fore they ever moved to this part of the country."

KUMPNY
Company.

"Jay, take this-here fresh towel an' hang it out yonder by the wash shelf 'cause we're gonna have kumpny an' it's a good time to start a clean one."

Overheard . . .
"He was a old man when I wasn't knee high to a grasshopper, so he has to be older than dirt."

◄ L ►

LARD
A soft white shortening obtained by rendering the fatty tissue of a hog.
"When we run out of hog lard, we buy a 50-pound stand if money ain't too tight, er a 8-pound bucket if it is."

LARRUPIN' GOOD
Very good tasting.
"I tell you one thang: that fried chicken of Misseries Carter's was larrupin' good."

'LASSES
Molasses.
"In cold weather 'lasses would git so thick that they'd bend a spoon handle tryin' to dip um out. Mamma use to heat um up on the stove so they'd pour jist as easy as Karo sirp."

LATCH STRING
A string used to lift an inside door latch from the outside; it can be pulled to the inside, thus preventing entrance from the outside.
"The latch string will always be out fer you—you are always welcome to my house."

LAY BY
The last cultivation of crops for the season.
"I use to lay by 'fore the Fourth but now hit's nearly August when I git done."

LAY IT ON
Blame it on.
"Murray wasn't no more guilty of that holdup than I am. They jist had to find somebody to lay it on."

LAY OFF
Mark or measure off.
"I'm gonna lay off the garden first thang in the mornin'."

LEARN
Teach.

"Miss Hern was the best to learn me somethin' of e're one of the teachers I had."

LAUNDRY AND IRONING

Mondays was wash day if it wasn't rainin' an' Tuesdays was arnin' day. Washpots an' tubs was set up close to the sprang er well, 'cause more water was used that day than any other, an' it all had to be dipped out of the sprang er drawed out of the well.

Clothes was biled in a big old arn washpot with the three legs set on rocks to git it high enough off of the ground so a good farr could be built under it. Slivers was shaved off of a cake of lye soap into the bilin' water, an' the clothes was punched an' stirred with a broom handle. After the clothes was biled good they was lifted over into a washtub an' scrubbed good on a washboard with more lye soap.

After the bilin' an' scrubbin' they was put through three tubs of clear, cool rench water. All the white thangs was finally run through rench water with bluein' in it to make um real white. Ever'thang was wrung out by twistin' um by hand. Them sheets was the hardest to wring out an' it was hard to keep um from touchin' the ground. Finally they was clothesline dried an' sunned.

Arnin' day was about the same amount of work an' in the summertime it was a mighty hot job. The arns had to be heated on top of the cookin' stove an' there wasn't no fans neither. Ever'thang from snot rags to bed sheets was sprinkled an' arned an' a lot of thangs was starched too. While one arn was bein' used there was three er four more a-heatin' on the stove. All that stove wood wasn't wasted jist on arnin' though—there'd be a pot of beans er taters on top of the stove an' maybe a pone of cornbread in the oven.

LEARNT
Taught.

"Miss Price tried to learn me to read but never done it, then whenever I got Misseries Roberts she shore-nuff learnt me good."

LEAST
Smallest, youngest.

"Sows has jist got twelve tits an' ourn jist had a litter of thirteen. The least one woulda starved, so Papa give it to me to raise."

LEASTWISE
Anyway.

"When the preacher come last Sunday we had some shore-nuff good kind of cake . . . leastwise they said it was."

LEAVE OUT FROM HERE
An order to leave.

"Mr. Berryhill's old cow is out yonder in my garden. Git your slingshot an' make her leave out from here."

'LECTION
Election.

"I ain't paid my poll tax yet, but I'm shore goin' to so I can vote in the next 'lection an' vote out that Republican they got in thar now."

'LECTRISTY
Electricity.

"I read in the *Times* whir folks way out in the country'll have 'lectristy in another five years' time."

LEGGERNS
A covering (as of leather or cloth) for the leg used for show and/or protection, leggings.

"Lots of men use to wear leather leggerns and ridin' britches, especially police, but not much no more."

LESS
Let's.

"Less me an' you go down yonder to the sprang an' lay down on our bellies an' drank out of it like we was horses."

LESSEN
Unless.
"They's allus a big bunch comes lessen it rains."

LET ON
Divulged, implied, said.
"I knowed which one of um done it but I never let on that I did."

LET OUT
The end of an activity, such as school, church, or a movie.
"By the time the pitcher show let out it was slap dark."

LET THE CAT OUT OF THE BAG
To give away the secret.
"They wouldn't uv nobody never knowed about it if blabber-mouth Wanda hadn't let the cat out of the bag."

LIABLE TO
Likely to.
"We're liable to git another gully-washer this evenin'."

LIBERRY
Library.
"I know what's in ever book in ever liberry in the whole world—words."

LICK AND A PROMISE
A hurried, slipshod job.
"I ain't got time to clean up the house; I'll jist have to give it a lick and a promise."

Overheard . . .
"Jim never gits a word in edgeways 'cause his old woman has got a tongue that's loose at both ends."

LICK OF
Bit of.
"J.P.'s so durn lazy he'd near bout starve 'fore he'd do a lick of work."

LIGHT A SHUCK
Hurry.
> "If you're gonna git them chickens fed 'fore they go to roost, you'd better light a shuck."

LIGHT BREAD
Store-bought bread that is light in weight as compared to biscuits or corn bread.
> "The onliest day we ever had light bread was on the Fourth of July whenever we'd buy goat stew to take home with us."

LIGHT INTO
To begin with haste.
> "I'm gonna light into that arnin' first thang an' git it done 'fore it gits too hot."

LIGHTNIN' BUGS
Fireflies.
> "The young-uns'd all git cut feet an' stumped toes tryin' to ketch lightnin' bugs of a night."

LIGHTS
Lungs, especially of a slaughtered animal.
> "Elmer killed hogs yistiddy an' he brung us a big mess of liver an' lights."

LIKE TO HAVE
Almost, nearly.
> "I like to have busted my sides laughin' at *Amos 'n Andy* the other night on the radio."

LISTEN AT
Listen to.
> "Mr. Winn allus looks at the radio when he's listenin' at it, says he can hear it plainer."

LIT
Landed.
> "I seen that-there airplane make two er three circles an' then it lit in Mr. Jordon's field. They said the driver-he was a barnstormer named Roscoe Turner an' he tuck folks up in that contraption fer fifty cents."

LIT OUT
Left.
> "After he got Judy in a family way he jist lit out an' they ain't nobody never seen hide ner hair of him since."

LITTLE SHAVER
A small child; quoted from one of Burma-Shave's signs in 1939:
> **"Past schoolhouses . . . take it slow.**
> **Let the little shavers grow. . . . BURMA-SHAVE."**
> "Last time I seen this young-un he was jist a little shaver."

LOADSTONE
Magnet.
> "A lot of times young-uns'd git a-holt of a loadstone out of a Model T magneto. They was shaped like a V."

LOCKJAW
Tetanus.
> "A girl that was a-playin' hide an' whoop in some thick dog fennel stepped on a piece of old rusty stovepipe an' took lockjaw an' died."

LOLLYGAG
Talk in an idle manner, dawdle.
> "He ain't never done nothin' but lollygag over at the store an' play checkers an' spit tobacker juice."

LONEY DOG
Baloney, bologna.
> "Give me a dime slice of loney dog, some sody crackers an' pepper sauce, a Moon Pie, an' a bottle of strawberry bellywash."

LONG AND LANKY
Tall and slender.
> "One time we had a principal at school that was long and lanky jist like Abe Lincoln, an' looked like him too."

LONG HANDLES or JOHNS
Warm underwear with long legs and sleeves.
> "In the summer we didn't wear nothin' under our overalls but when cold weather would come along ever'body'd put on them long handles."

LONG TOM
A gun with a very long barrel.
"Grandpa toted a 36-inch long tom 12-gauge that would knock a squirrel out of the tallest tree in the woods."

LOOK-A-HERE
Look.
"Look-a-here, I've got a fish on my line an' I thank he's a big one."

LOOKED DOWN ON
Thought to be substandard by those with greater-than-thou attitudes.
"Except fer bein' as pore as Job's turkey, them Pendletons ain't no diff'runt from nobody else. I don't see why they're looked down on."

Overheard . . .
"My yonder-way neighbor makes me mad enough fer my rifle's trigger to itch."

LOOKED LIKE
Seemed.
"Them clouds back yonder in the southwest was mighty boogery. Looked like there might uv been a toynader in amoungst um."

LOOK FOR
Expect.
I look for it to fair off by dinner."

LOOKING GLASS
Mirror.
"Gertrude is so ugly that I bet she ain't never looked in no looking glass in her life, but if she did I bet she never looked again."

LOPIN'
Leaping or bounding gait of a horse or mule.
"Leon was ridin' bareback on that lopin' old mule when he fell off. She never throwed him like he claimed."

LOST MY HEAD
Became very angry.
"I wouldn't uv slapped Naomi fer nothin', but I jist lost my head."

'LOW
Allow, consider, be of the opinion.
"Don't you 'low hit might rain 'fore night?"

Overheard . . .
"Hit's the latest I've ever knowed it to be in my life."

◀ M ▶

MAD AS FARR
Very angry.

"Whenever them judges hands out, say, a five-year sentence, an' another'n on top of that, then says the feller can serve both of them at the same time, it jist make me mad as farr. A body kain't get paid fer two jobs if he ain't doin' but one, an' that's the same thang."

MADE A HABIT OF
Something done with regularity.

"Wilbur has gone an' made a habit of bein' jist as despisable as he can make hisself."

MADE NO BONES ABOUT IT
Made no pretense.

"Larry jist up an' told Wally he was a bald-faced liar an' was a low-down rotten snake an' he never made no bones about it."

MADE UP
Fabricated.

"Naomi got a hunderd on the story she made up in school."

MAIL RIDER
Rural mail carrier.

"Go meet the mail rider an' git me two three-cent stamps an' a penny post card an' don't git um sweaty er dirty er lose um ner nothin'."

MAKE
Mature, produce.

"My corn's done started curlin', an' if we don't git a rain mighty soon it ain't a-gonna make."

MAKE A BRANCH
Urinate.

"Stop the wagon fer a minute. I've got to step down an' make a branch."

MAKE LIGHT OF
Belittle, make fun of.
> "The folks that lived in town use to make light of the country girls that had to wear flour an' fertilizer sack dresses to school."

MAKE MUSIC
Play a musical instrument.
> "I use to make music fer square dainces."

MAKE OUT LIKE
Pretend.
> "Let's make out like you was the daddy an' I was the mamma."

MAKE OVER
Brag about, compliment.
> "Elvin allus seems to make over his littlest one but he shore don't the balance of um."

MAKES NO NEVERMIND
Makes no difference, doesn't matter.
> "Whichever one of them pups you want, you can have. It makes no nevermind to me."

Overheard . . .
"Why, she's so skinny that if she drunk a bottle of strawberry bellywash she'd look like a thermometer."

MAKE TRACKS
Get going, leave.
> "If a man kain't act like an' talk like a gentleman around my womenfolks, he better be ready to make tracks in a quick hurry."

MAKE YOU A PRESENT OF
Give you.
> "Bein' as how you like that little doily so good, I'll jist make you a present of it."

MAKIN' EYES
Flirting.

"Looks like Sue's done set her cap fer Fred; I seen her makin' eyes at him at the corn shuckin'."

MANY A ONE
Several.

"I've worked all day from can to kain't fer fifty cents an' dinner, many a one."

MANY'S THE TIME
Often.

"Them schoolboys from town would have them good old baloney an' light bread sandwiches. Many's the time I wished I had one of um instead of my aig er a sausage er a piece of country ham in a biscuit."

MARRED
Mired.

"The wagon got marred down to the hub in that mud hole an' the mule jist balked, so Otis had to build a farr under that mule to make him move. Well, he moved all right, but jist fer enough to whir the wagon got burnt up."

MARVELS
Marbles.

"At recess we play with our tops an' yoyos an' shoot marvels."

MASH
Push.

"When you want a car to go, you mash on the gas, an' if you want it to stop, you mash the brake."

MATERS
Tomatoes.

"I do love taters, maters, an' okry."

MAUD-MULE
A female or mare mule (hybrid).

"The pullin'est thang I ever seen was a big old 17-hand maud-mule at the fair."

MAUL
The drumstick of a fowl.
> "My sister liked the pully bone, I liked the maul, Mamma liked the neck an' feet, an' Daddy jist liked chicken."

MEADOW MUFFIN
A pile of cow dung.
> "Take care you don't 'cut your foot' on a meadow muffin out thar in that pasture."

MEAN AS A SNAKE
About as mean as one can get.
> "They jist wasn't nobody that could git along with old man Nash; he was as mean as a snake."

MENDIN'
1. Recovering from illness.
> "Lizzie is finally mendin' a little, but she still ain't right real peart."

2. Gaining weight.
> "I told Ersula she looked real good since she started mendin' a mite, an' it made her plumb mad that I said it."

MERE
Mirror.
> "I'd say Bessie ain't never wore out no mere."

MIDDLIN'
Mediocre.
> "I ain't been feelin' better'n middlin' since I had that bad spell last fall."

MIDDLIN' OF MEAT
A side of bacon.
> "Whenever I holp Calvin kill, scald, scrape, gut, an' cut up them four hogs of hisn, he give me a middlin' of meat fer my trouble."

MIFFED
Offended, mildly angered.
> "Misseries Mathis was miffed when I led her Jimbo home by the ear, but the overbearin' bully wouldn't let the other young-uns have nothin' to play with."

MIGHT COULD
Probably could.
>"I might could git done by night if it don't rain."

MIGHT NEAR
Nearly, almost.
>"It was so hot in that church that I might near fainted."

MIND
Obey.
>"It's got to whir young-uns ain't made to mind, an' some of um even talk back to their folks."

MINNER
Minnow.
>"The fish that John caught looked like a minner compared to the one Nadine pulled in, an' he never tuck her with him no more."

MISSERIES
Mrs.
>"I went over an' holp Misseries Varner put up her beans today."

MIZ
Mrs.; an abbreviated form of Misseries.
>"I never quite caught whir it was Miss er Miz, ma'am, but if you've got a man we'd be proud to have him come too."

MOANBACK
Come on back.
>"Cut her both ways an' moanback."

MONKEYSHINE
A playful trick, prank.
>"He was the funniest thang I ever seen. He pulled one monkeyshine right after the other'n."

MONTH OF SUNDAYS
A very long time.
>"George, whir in the world you been? I ain't seen you in a month of Sundays."

MOONSHINE
Illegally distilled corn whiskey, often called *shine* or *white lightning* or, if of inferior quality, *rot gut.*
"Mr. Ramsey never made no rot-gut whiskey. He turned out the best moonshine in the whole county."

Overheard . . .
"He squinted into his memory."

MORE THAN CARTER'S GOT LIVER PILLS
An expression meaning a huge amount.
"Whenever a feller wants to tell about a-havin' a whole heap of somethin', they'll say they've got more of it than Carter's got liver pills."

MORE THAN YOU COULD STIR WITH A STICK
An expression meaning many.
"If half the folks that turned out fer the rally give Herman their vote, he'll go in. I never seen sitch a mob—more than you could stir with a stick."

MORTIFIED
Shocked, surprised, embarrassed.
"When I heard that Lurleen had married the town drunk, I was jist plumb mortified."

MOSEY
Amble, stroll.
"I reckin I'll mosey on over to that patch of woods an' see if I can shoot me a squirrel."

MOSQUITO BAR
A fine net or screen used to keep out mosquitos.
"Fix up somethin' over the baby's crib that will hold a mosquito bar up so it won't fall through on him."

MOSQUITO HAWK
Dragon fly, snake doctor.
"Y'all can call them thangs a mosquito hawk if you're of a mind to, but they ain't nothin' but a old snake doctor."

MOUGHT
Might.
> "If my crops make good I jist mought buy the old woman a new set of wash tubs."

MOUNTAIN OYSTERS
Boar or bull testicles.
> "I eat some mountain oysters one time an' liked them real good, but I never knowed what they was 'fore I eat um."

MOUNTING
Mountain.
> "Heered tell of a feller that lived way off on a mounting sommers by hisself fer so long he plumb forgot how to talk."

MOUTH
The "voice" of a hunting dog.
> "Old Queenie has, beyond a doubt, got the best mouth of any hound I've ever heered in my life."

MOUTH ORGAN or HARP
Harmonica.
> "One of the young-uns can play a mouth organ real good but the other'n kain't play nothin' but a radio."

MUCH OBLIGED
An expression of appreciation.
> "I'm much obliged to you fer doin' fer us when we was down with the flu."

Overheard . . .
"Luvonia's new feller looks as silly as a calf a-starin' at a new gate."

MUCH OBLIGED TILL YOU'RE BETTER PAID
An expression meaning accept my thanks for now, until I can find a way to repay you.
> "If you hadn't gone after the doctor for Veeta, she jist might not uv made it. I'm shore much obliged till you're better paid."

> *Overheard . . .*
> "Royce's sitch a liar he has to git somebody else to call his hogs fer him."

MUCH OF A MAN
A very large, very strong man.
"Z.B. could lift an' tote them 200-pound fertilize sacks all day long. He was much of a man."

MY-NAISE
Mayonnaise.
"I like to go pick me a big ripe tomato right out of the garden, while the dew is still on it, put some my-naise, salt and pepper on it, and eat it right on the spot."

NAIRN, NARY
Not a one, never a one, none.
"A bunch of the boys at school has got yoyos but I ain't got nairn."

NAR
Narrow.
"Floyd was a right quare lookin' feller. His eyebrows come together, an' he was real nar between the eyes."

NASTY
1. Disgustingly filthy.
"Fran shore keeps a nasty house."
2. Indecent, obscene.
"I ain't never seen nobody that acts an' talks as nasty as Pete does."

NAW
No.
"Naw, I ain't goin' to have no blind date. I might let her git hurt 'cause I ain't used to blind folks."

Overheard . . .
"If Elvin ever catches anybody a-messin' with his stuff, he'll jump on him like a duck on a June bug."

NEAR BOUT
Nearly, almost.
"Yep, I near bout married that red-headed woman till I found out that at least a dozen men knowed her a whole lot better'n I did."

NECK AND EARS
From the shoulders up, excepting hair.
"Take this-here wash rag an' wash your neck and ears real good 'fore you go to school."

NECKID
Naked.
"Jim went in a-washin' in the creek neckid an' somebody come by an' tuck all his clothes."

NER
Neither, nor.
"They was about the same dumb. Ner one of um knowed his nose from a hole in the ground."

NEVER
Didn't.
"She told Mamma I done it but I never neither."

NEVER HEARD TELL OF
Never heard of.
"I never heard tell of sitch a long dry spell like we're havin'. Why, they's bullfrogs as big as shoats that ain't never seen water."

NEVER MIND
Ignore, disregard.
"Never mind him. He don't know what he's talkin' about nohow."

NEW GROUND
Newly cleared land.
"Ben's over yonder grubbin' sprouts in the new ground."

NEW YORK MINUTE
A very short jiffy, much less than 60 seconds.
"When I seen that bull a-comin' after me, I was under the fence in a New York minute."

NIGH ONTO
Nearly.
"I reckin he's nigh onto 80 year old an' he's jist as feisty as ever."

NIGHT COMIN' ON
Darkness setting in.
"With night comin' on, the shurf called off the search till mornin'."

NO COUNT
No good.

"That no count gun snapped on me agin, er I'd uv had me a rabbit."

NOHOW
Anyhow.

"Milford don't have to put up with his boss a-treatin' him like dirt. He's pretty well fixed an' don't have to work nohow."

NOPE
No.

"Marvin offered me a drank of his old rot gut whiskey, an' I told him, 'Nope, I reckin not, I hardly ever drank.'"

NOT A THING LIKE
No resemblance.

"Dewatha is not a thing like her sister Corine. They're as diff'runt as daylight and dark."

NO TELLIN', AIN'T NO TELLIN'
There is no way of knowing.

"No tellin' how much his daddy's spent a-gittin' that sorry boy out of trouble."

NOTHIN' TO IT
Untrue, of little substance.

"Diff'runt ones has said that when Norris was gone so long that he was in the lock-up, but there's nothin' to it. I found out he was a-workin' up North at a car tar place the whole three years."

NOTHIN' TO WRITE HOME ABOUT
Nothing very exciting or significant.

"I've allus heered that California was the best place there ever was, but I don't thank it's nothin' to write home about."

NOTHIN' WOULD DO HER
She wouldn't be satisfied.

"Doris had her a good man but nothin' would do her but to start messin' around with ever Tom, Dick, an' Harry till he got a bait of it an' left her."

NOT TOO FAR FROM NOW
Before long.
"They're gonna pass a law not too far from now whir the womenfolks will git to vote same as men. You jist mark my word."

NOT WORTH HIS SALT
Not worth the value of the salt one consumes.
"That feller they hard to take Luke's place is jist not worth his salt."

NOW AND AGIN
Once in a while.
"I still see Betty now and agin but not regular no more."

NUBBIN
An immature ear of corn.
"Looks like my corn ain't gonna make more'n one nubbin to the stalk."

Overheard . . .
"I've got ever'thang I want, but sometimes I have to shave my wantin' perty close."

◄ O ►

OF A EVENIN'
In the evening.
"I went to see Clair down in Floridy an' didn't like it much. I'm use to a-settin' out of a evenin' but them dratted skeeters'll eat you alive."

OF A MIND TO
1. Care to.
"Come along with me an' Jim if you're of a mind to."
2. In the frame of mind to.
"I'm of a mind to give you a thrashin' fer doin' that."

OFF AND ON
Every once in a while, occasionally.
"Martha's had bad colds er some kind of kain't-help-its off and on all winter."

OKRY
Okra.
"You can take okry an' fix it any way you're of a mind to an' I'll allus eat a bait of it."

OLD DOGS BARK A-SETTIN' DOWN
With age comes the wisdom of conserving energy.
"It's true that old dogs bark a-settin' down. They figger that whatever they're a-barkin' at can hear them jist as good as they could if they run to it."

OLD HOME PLACE
Where one grew up, and in most cases, where one was born.
"If it hadn't been fer the well, I never could uv found the old home place."

OLD WOMAN
Wife, or in some cases, mother.
"Me an' the old woman raised six head of young-uns an' never lost a one."

OLD-FASHIONED CLOTHING

Mamma didn't have no store-bought dress till she was 38 year old. Women's an' girl's clothes was allus sewed by hand er on a foot-operated treadle sewin' machine. Some women was a good hand at makin' shirts too, but overalls, shoes, an' stockin's had to be bought.

If folks had a little money they could buy yard goods fer makin' dresses an' stuff, but durin' hard times most of the dresses was made out of flour an' fertilize sacks. It got to whir flour'd come in sacks that had perty flowers an' checks on um. Girls allus wore bonnets a-workin' out in the fields er gardens. They was homemade an' had a stiff bill (visor) in front an' a ruffle in back to protect the neck. Strangs tied under the chin kept it on in the wind. Women'd wear stockin's over their hands an' arms with fanger holes cut in um. It was a awful thang fer women to let the sun darken their skin. They wanted to be "fair as a lily an' slim as a dirt dobber."

Six-inch brogan shoes was fer workin' in an' wearin' to school in the wintertime but you jist got one pair a year. Children's shoes was usually bought a size too large 'cause their feet grew so fast they soon was wearin' pinchin' shoes. Jist grown folks wore shoes in the summertime. Slippers, if you had any, was fer wearin' to church an' Sunday school. Whenever the soles er heels wore out, new ones was cut an' nailed on at home.

ONE OR THE TWO
One or the other.

"Nadine told Ralph he had to give up gittin' drunk or her one. It had to be one or the two."

ON HIS OWN HOOK
On his own initiative.

"Claude wants me to go on the halves with him to buy some biddies to raise up an' sell um, but he never comes out on anythang. If he wants to raise fryers he'll jist have to do it on his own hook."

ONLIEST
Only.
>"If it wasn't the onliest one I've got I'd jist make you a present of it."

ON THE DOT
Exactly on time.
>"I jist love to listen at Lum an' Abner on that-there batt'ry radio. They come on at six o'clock, right on the dot."

ON THE HALVES
Fifty-fifty.
>"We went in on the halves an' bought that bull."

OODLES
A considerable amount.
>"Kate married well off. Her man has jist got oodles of money, they say."

OPSIT
On the other side, across from.
>"Geneva here, she does good in her books, but Tonnis is jist the opsit. He's about to fail."

ORT TO, ORTA
Should.
>"I ort to have three dozen aigs to trade by the time the peddlin' wagon comes."

OURN
Ours.
>"We ain't got much but what we've got is ourn an' it wasn't give to us."

OUTEN
Out of.
>"That old quilt was made outen scraps from old dresses goin' way back to 'fore the war."

OUT OF HEARIN'
A distance beyond one's ability to hear.
>"Them coon dogs went plumb out of hearin', then they doubled back to within fifty yards of whir we was."

OUT OF WHACK
Doesn't function.
  "My old Ford's out of whack an' we'll jist have to foot it till I can git it fixed."

OUTSIDE WOMEN
Girl friends of a married man.
  "Some day Gertrude's gonna find out about all them outside women that Stan's got."

OVAIR
Over there.
  "Bessie went ovair to the dress factory an' they hard her to sew fer them the same day."

OVALLS or OVERHALLS
Overalls.
  "Ovalls is sorta like britches 'cept they've got a bib in the front an' gallowses to hold um up, an' a heap more pockets."

OVERBALANCED
Loss of balance.
  "I couldn't work on one of them towers, 'cause I'm too bad to git overbalanced."

OVER YONDER
Over there.
  "I had two boys to go over yonder in the big war."

Overheard . . .
"It was so dark you had to strike a second match to see if the first one was lit."

◄ P - Q ►

PAINTER
Panther.
> "They say a painter sounds jist like a screamin' woman, but I ain't never heered one myself."

PALIN'
Fence pale or picket.
> "I wish I had me a palin' fence around the house so I could keep them dadburn chickens out."

PALLET
A temporary bed, usually made on the floor.
> "Y'all jist stay all night; we got a extry bed an' we can make a big pallet fer the young-uns."

Overheard . . .
"If it don't rain it'll miss a mighty good chainct."

PALMETTO or SWAMP CABBAGE
The heart of a palmetto palm, delicious cooked or raw.
> "Lots of folks say swamp cabbage tastes the same as regular cabbage, but I don't."

PARASOL
Umbrella.
> "I reckin they ain't nobody had no use fer no parasol ner nothin' to keep um from gittin' wet lately. It's been sitch a long dry spell they say the Suwannee River's done shet down to a three-day week."

PARCHED
Roasted.
> "Bernice likes parched peanuts but she kain't stand um biled."

PARTIAL TO
Give or gave preference to.
> "I was allus partial to Kentucky Wonder pole beans myself."

PASSEL
Parcel, bunch.
"I know whir you can git a-holt of some guineas. A feller by the name of Willin'ham over on Moose River's got a whole passel of um fer sale."

PASS SOME TIME
Visit, loaf.
"Last Sunday evenin' me an' Jim went off down in the holler jist to pass some time."

Overheard . . .
"It used to be folks worked till the lightnin' bugs started blinkin'."

PASS WORDS
Squabble.
"We lived with my Mamma-in-law fer the first year an' never did pass words."

PASTEBOARD
Cardboard.
"Kain't hardly find no wooden boxes no more; all you can git is pasteboard."

PASTER
Pasture.
"Mr. Barnett give Daddy a place to live, a garden spot, a paster fer the cow, an' ten dollars a month."

PAST GOIN'
Unable to move about on one's own.
"This old arthuritus has jist about got me past goin'."

PAY NO MIND
Pay no attention, ignore.
"Pay no mind to what them politicians say they're gonna do. They git mighty forgetful after they git put in."

PAYTROTIC
Patriotic.
> "I don't thank nobody ort to git hard on no givement job, ner be give no givement hand-outs neither, if he ain't paytrotic."

PEAK-ED
Pale or sick looking.
> "That young-un looks mighty peak-ed; let me feel of his fard."

PEART
Lively.
> "I sent after the doctor an' he's had Doris in bed fer a week, but he's got her a-lookin' right peart agin."

PEARTENIN' JUICE
Whiskey.
> "At the corn shuckin's they'd bury a jug of peartenin' juice sommers in the pile of corn an' the one that found it got to drank the most."

PECKERWOOD
Woodpecker.
> "Travis' teacher wouldn't let him call a woodpecker a peckerwood an' it made him mad. That's what he'd allus called them."

PEDDLIN' WAGON
A covered wagon, stocked with items from a general store, made scheduled trips to the rural areas. Customers had little cash so they bartered for their needs with such items as eggs, chickens, and butter. After trucks became available, they became known as rollin' stores instead of peddlin' wagons.

PEN
Penitentiary.
> "Old Oscar Beddin'field jist got turned loose from pullin' a year an' a day in the pen."

PENDERS
Peanuts, goobers.
"What folks does is to plaint corn an' penders in the field together. When the corn is gathered they turn in feeder pigs to eat the corn that was left an' root up the penders, so by the time they root out the field they're fattened up fer butcherin'."

PEOPLE
Kin.
"His people was all farmers an' mine allus worked at public works."

PERLOW
Pilau, a dish made of seasoned rice and meat, usually chicken.
"They're fixin' a big slew of chicken perlow an' swamp cabbage over at the church."

PERSNICKETY
1. Fussy about small details.
"The teacher was real persnickety about ever'body stayin' between the lines on the tablet."
2. Snobbish, uppity.
"Marlene was real persnickety—thought she was better'n anybody else."

PERT NEAR
Almost but not quite.
"I'm glad I'm done with that job 'cause I'm pert near give out."

PERTY
Pretty.
"Organdy makes a mighty perty dress but it wrinkles awful bad."

PERTY COME OFF
Expression similar to "hell of a note."
"It's a perty come off when even the preacher gits caught in the jenny barn."

PETER OUT
Become exhausted.
"I'm gonna go over an' set in the shade a spell, I'm about to peter out."

PETTED
Spoiled, catered to.
"Jim was awful hard on them boys but he allus petted the girls."

PICAYUNISH
Hard to please.
"Doreen's kids is so picayunish about their eatin' I don't know what to fix for dinner."

PIECE
Join together, splice.
"If a young-un's dress got too short, Mamma'd jist piece it."

PIECE A SQUARE
Hand sewing a square to become part of a quilt top.
"Mamma'd take a old sack of rags and piece quilt squares as perty as anybody's."

PIED-ED
Two or more colors.
"That pied-ed cow ain't nothin' to look at, but she shore fills the milk bucket."

PIE PLANT
Rhubarb.
"Pie plant is perty easy to grow an' they ain't nothin' that's better fer makin' a pie."

PIKE
Turnpike, highway.
"Whir the old log road use to be they's a nice pike there now."

PILLER
Pillow.
"Them pillers was filled with breast feathers from Clara's geese."

PINT
Point.
"Looks like to me that preacher likes to pint his fanger right at me when he's a-preachin'."

PITCHER
Picture.
"She's as perty as a pitcher."

PITCHER SHOW
Picture show, movie.
"By the time a body takes his gal to the pitcher show, buys a hamburger an' Dope at the drive-in an' three gallons of gas, he's done spent more'n three dollars cash money."

PITCHIN' A FIT
1. Throwing a tantrum.
"Mamma use to call pitchin' a fit a ground fit."
2. Expressing impatience or expectation.
"Dean was jist pitchin' a fit to go to the ball game but had done spent his money."

PIZEN
Poison.
"A old spreadin' adder is jist as pizen as a rattlesnake, they tell me."

P'LIKE, PLAY LIKE
Pretend.
"Less go down yonder in the woods whir all them grape vines is an' swang on um an' p'like we was Tarzan."

PLAINT
Plant.
"Looks like I'm gonna have to plaint my corn agin, 'cause I didn't git no good stand."

PLANK
A large board.
"The floor planks in that house had cracks so big you could see the chickens under the floor."

PLATTED
Braided.
"Grown women with platted hair jist don't look right to me."

PLAYED OUT
Used up, worn out, ceases to operate satisfactorily.
"I'm goin' to have to git me another car, I reckin. My old Tin Lizzie is jist about played out."

PLAY PERTY
1. Toy, usually homemade.
"I'm a-workin' on you a play perty fer your birthday."
2. A caution to children to be nice to one another while playing.
"If y'all don't play perty, I ain't goin' to let you play together no more this week."

PLEASURED
Pleased, gave satisfaction or joy.
"I've allus pleasured in havin' fresh garden stuff more'n any kind of meat there ever was."

PLEESE
Police.
"They jist got one pleese, Slim Wilson, an' he mostly ketches speeders on his motorsickle."

PLUMB
Completely.
"Don't fill the bucket plumb full er it'll splash out on you when you tote it."

POKE
Paper sack.
"If you'll put them two little pokes in that big one it'll be easier fer me to tote the coal oil can."

POOCHED OUT
Protruded.
"It made him so mad he turned red an' pooched out his lips."

POORLY
Ailing, sickly.
"Becky has been feelin' poorly but she's a-gittin' better, I thank."

POOT
To release gas rectally, to break wind.
"Never set in the show with Elvin Wallace. He eats pinto beans, onions, biled aigs, an' cabbage, an' when he lets a poot it will gag you an' make your eyes water."

POP KNOT
A knot on the head caused by getting hit with a hard object.
"Tonnis got hit on the head with a bat an' it raised a big old pop knot."

POPPIN' THE QUESTION
Proposing marriage.
"I've jist got a feelin' that Leroy's gonna be poppin' the question any day now."

PORE
Poor.
"I knowed a family one time that was so pore that when their mule died they couldn't buy another'n an' the feller's old lady an' his pore little young-uns had to pull the plow."

PORE AS JOB'S TURKEY
Exceedingly poor.
"We was allus as pore as Job's turkey but we managed to eat ever day."

PORE LAND
Infertile land.
"He's tryin' to scratch out a livin' on that old pore rocky land."

POT KAIN'T CALL THE KITTLE BLACK
An expression meaning one is no better than the other.
"Dewatha goes barefoot, don't wear no drawers, cusses an' dips snuff, but Veota helps make shine, lays up with men, an' don't know what the inside of a church looks like. The pot kain't call the kittle black."

POT LIKKER
The liquid left in a pot after cooking.
"I like to crumble up corn bread in pot likker an' eat nothin' but that fer supper till I git a bellyful."

POTRIGE
Partridge.
"Most folks know a potrige better by another name—quail."

Overheard . . .
"I allus dreaded climbin' a hill steeper than straight up."

POULTICE
A soft, usually medicated, mass spread on cloth and applied to sores or other lesions.
"I allus hated havin' a mustard poultice tied on my chest."

PRECIOUS LITTLE
Very little.
"It's got to whir, even if a body has a little money, there's precious little it'll buy."

PRISE POLE
Pry pole.
"Willis never did haul no car jack. Whenever he had a flat tar he'd jist find him a saplin' er a fence post an' use it fer a prise pole."

PROB'LY
Probably.
"Jess'll prob'ly end up marryin' that gal what works down yonder at that jook, an' it'll be like goin' from the fryin' pan into the farr if he does."

PROP POLE
A stick or board used near the center of a span of clothes line to take the sag out when wet clothes are hung on it.
"Jist about ever clothes line has a sag an' has to have a prop pole put under it."

PROUD
1. Pleased, happy.
"I'm proud you got a A on your report card."
2. Pride, self-respect.
"We ain't never had much, but our folks has allus been proud."

PUDDLE JUMPER
A small car or one with all, or most all, of its body removed, as a skeeter.
"Some folks call Ben's old Ford a puddle jumper but I call it a skeeter."

PUKE
Vomit.
"It nearly makes me puke jist to thank about eatin' raw oysters."

PULLED BOTH EARS BACK
Pulled both hammers back on a double-barreled shotgun.
"When Cecil saw that big buck slippin' through the bushes he pulled both ears back on his old 12-gauge. When he pulled the trigger fer the right barrel the left one fired too—nearly broke his shoulder."

PULLED OUT
Left.
"One day he jist up an' pulled out."

PULLIN' FODDER
Stripping mature leaves from corn stalks to be used as animal feed.
"Pullin' fodder ain't hardly as bad as pickin' cotton, but nearly."

PULL TIME
Serve a jail or prison sentence.
"Arnold's daddy is well off an' allus pays him out of trouble. He ain't never had to pull time."

PULLY BONE
Wish bone.
"How about me an' you breakin' the pully bone to see which one gits his wish?"

PUNCHIN' DOCTOR
A chiropractor.
"I thank that punchin' doctor done me more good than that pill doctor."

PUNY
Weak.
"He's smart but he's jist too puny to do much work."

PUSH COMES TO SHOVE
When a difficult situation becomes even more difficult.
> "I never did like the idy of workin' fer the other feller, but if push comes to shove I might have to."

PUSSLE-GUTTED
Fat.
> "I wouldn't uv knowed Leroy. I ain't seen him in ten year an' he's done got plumb pussle-gutted."

PUT IN TO
Started, commenced.
> "Dizzy ain't got a lick of sense. Soon as he got his divorce he put in to writin' to them women that was advertisin' in the paper fer a husband."

PUT IT DOWN IN GRANDMA, GRANNY GEAR
Shift to the vehicle's lowest gear, generally the first of five.
> "My old truck was loaded mighty heavy, an' comin' over Possum Trot Hill I had to put it down in grandma."

PUT ON AIRS
A display of one's importance or wealth, usually false.
> "Ain't no tellin' what kind of folks them Thorntons is 'cause they allus put on airs so much you kain't tell much about um."

PUT ON THE FEED BAG
To eat, derived from tying a feed bag, which is sized and shaped for the purpose, over a horse's mouth so that he may eat while working.
> "By the time we git back to the house it'll be time to put on the feed bag an' I'm ready fer it. My guts has been a-growlin' fer a hour."

PUTS ME IN THE MIND OF
Reminds me of.
> "Pete puts me in the mind of your daddy when he was jist a sprout of a boy."

PUTTIN' ON
Pretending, acting.
> "James wasn't hurt hardly at all, he was jist puttin' on 'cause that perty girl was holdin' his head in her lap."

> *Overheard . . .*
> "Look at Hank in his new Palm Beach suit an' Panama hat—he's as proud as a dog with two tails."

PUTTIN' ON THE DOG
Showing off, by wearing fancy clothes, using big words, being an exhibitionist, or acting important.
"The way George is puttin' on the dog you'd thank he was a millionaire, but he ain't never had more'n two quarters to rub together."

PUT UP
To preserve food, usually called "canning" even though using glass jars.
"Misseries Bennett's got over 200 quarts of stuff in her storm cellar that she put up last sprang."

PUT UP WITH
Tolerate.
"Doris has to put up with Melvin's bird dogs a-howlin' all night an' her so bad off."

QUARE
Queer.
"He's as quare as a chicken hatched in a thunderstorm."

QUILED
Coiled.
"That big old snake was all quiled up a-fixin' to strike."

QUITE A SPELL
A long time.
"I reckin Mr. Blanchard's folks is a-doin' all right, but I ain't seen um in quite a spell."

◄ R ►

RACKET
Noise, sound.
"Fred can pick up jist about anythang with strangs on it an' make a perty good racket."

RAIL
Real.
"Doris use to have these rail bad sick headaches till she went to that new punchin' doctor an' he done away with um."

RAILROAD TIME
Correct time.
"Railroad time is all right if you're runnin' a railroad, but I jist tell time by the sun an' that's close enough fer me."

RAISED
Reared.
"When young-uns ain't raised right they ain't got much of a chaince of turnin' out good. Then agin, some will go aginst their raisin' an' turn out to be rotten apples anyhow."

RAISED ON CONCRETE
Brought up in the city.
"Dez's nephew didn't know a thang about dirt, that is, the farmin' kind, 'cause he'd been raised on concrete."

RAISED SAND
Raised hell.
"When Geneva caught Bo with another woman she shore raised sand but she never packed her duds."

Overheard . . .
"Yesterday was a week ago." (It really wasn't that long ago. A week ago yesterday is what is meant.)

RAMBLIN' FEVER
A desire to ramble or roam.
"Ever sprang when the weather turns good I git the ramblin' fever."

RAMPS
Edible wild plants that grow in the southeastern mountains during the spring, known as wild leeks or Indian onions.
"Ramps ain't fer ladies er fellers that go a-courtin' um. When a body eats them-there ramps the best thang he can do is to go off sommers by hisself fer a week er more 'cause they ain't nobody that can stand his breath."

Overheard . . .
". . . careful as porcupines makin' love."

RAMSHACKLED
1. Rickety, carelessly or loosely constructed.
"Jim an' Joan live in a mighty ramshackled old shack up on the side of a hill."
2. Ransacked.
"They hadn't been gone but two days an' their house was ramshackled an' ever'thang worth anythang was stold."

RAPSCALLION
Rascal, ne'er do well.
"That old rapscallion turned out to have a pile of money."

RARIN' TO GO
Anxious, impatient to begin.
"I'll have all my fishin' stuff an' coffee ready an' raring' to go by the time you git here in the mornin'."

RASHER
A thin slice or a portion consisting of such slices.
"I can take an' put a rasher of tomato an' one of onion between two slices of bread with a little my-naise an' have a mighty fine sandwich."

RATIONS
Food, provisions.
"I'm about out of rations an' they ain't no money in sight."

RAUNCHY
1. Filthy.
"I seen Gordon with about the most raunchy woman I've ever saw."
2. Obscene, smutty.
"Them jokes that they told at the show was jist too raunchy fer me."

RAWBONED
Having a coarse, heavy frame inadequately covered with flesh.
"Ever'one of them Chandler young-uns was right fleshy but Hubert. He turned out to be big an' rawboned an' ugly as a mud fence."

RAZORBACK
A thin-bodied, long-legged, long-snouted, half-wild mongrel hog.
"Sam's prize hound got tore all to pieces on that last razorback hunt. That big old boar had tusks two inches long."

RAZOR STROP
A band, usually leather, for sharpening a razor.
"Ever time I got a whuppin' it was with a peach tree limb er Daddy's razor strop. It was made from a piece of leather belt from a cotton mill."

READY-ROLLED
Already rolled cigarettes or "tailor-mades," as opposed to "roll-your-own."
"I never did smoke no ready-rolled cigarettes till I was about thirteen. I had tried smokin' rabbit tobacker, grape vines, corn silks, and chimley sut 'fore ever tryin' shore-nuff tobacker."

RECEIPT
Recipe.
"I've got to run down whoever made that carrot cake an' try to git the receipt fer it."

RECKIN
Reckon, suppose, think, believe, intend.
"I reckin them Republicans is goin' to send us all to the pore house."

RECOLLECT
Remember, recall.
"I recollect when a stout man couldn't hardly tote five dollars worth of rations."

RED BUG
Chigger, known to Florida Crackers as a red bug.
"It don't matter whir a body calls um a chigger er a red bug, they're powerful pizen."

REGIONAL PRONUNCIATIONS

One clue to the part of the country a person grew up in is his use of the R sound in speech. One knows that someone who "paaks the cah in the yaad" must be from Boston, from both the long A's and the missing R's. In the South (and in Boston too), a number of words have acquired a final R, sometimes being substituted for "a" and "o" as in Alabamer *(Alabama)*, banjer *(banjo)*, Cuber *(Cuba)*, Emmer *(Emma)*, holler *(hollow)*, minner *(minnow)*, tomater *(tomato)*, and winder *(window)*.

In contrast (to quote Mark Twain), "The EDUCATED Southerner has no use for an R except at the beginning of a word." Propah folks substitute "ah" for "er," as in mothah, preachah, heah, flowah, *and* rivah.

REG'LER
Regular.
"Whenever a feller starts seein' a gal right reg'ler, you can figger he's jist about a goner."

RENCH
Rinse.
"I allus use bluein' in my rench water to make thangs perty an' white."

RENDER
To melt down, extract by melting.
"Them old washpots git used fer washin' clothes, makin' soap, and renderin' lard too."

RETCH
Reached.
"Soon as the blessin' was ast, Hershel stood up in his cher, jist in his shirttail, an' retch plumb across the table fer a biscuit."

RID
Rode.
"I ain't never had a worser ride than when I rid Marvin's old mule to town bareback. It was like settin' on the edge of a two-by-four."

RIGHT
Very, extremely.
"My corn had done curled up, but day 'fore yistiddy we got a right good shower an' hit's a-comin' out now."

RIGHT AT
Almost.
"Old Tex Willin'ham is the highest off the ground of any man I've ever saw. He's right at seven foot."

RIGHT HAND RUNNIN'
In succession.
"Why, I've seen Duke eat as high as six big hen aigs right hand runnin' an' that many biscuits too."

RIGHT MANY
Several.
"They's right many rabbits a-eatin' up my garden, an' I'm gonna see how many number six shot they can tote off."

RIGHT MUCH
A lot.
"Paul said y'all got right much rain out your way last Tuesday."

RIGHT OFF THE BAT
Immediately.
> "Me an' Paul went out a-huntin' fer a bee tree, an' right off the bat we found a big one."

RIGHT SMART
Many, several, large.
> "They's a right smart bunch of um in the school that's got head lice an' the itch."

RILED
Angered, agitated, upset, irritated.
> "Folks say a rattler will allus rattle when he's riled and won't bite 'less he rattles first. I'll jist figger he's allus mad whir he rattles or not."

RING A CHICKEN'S NECK
Kill a chicken by holding its head and neck in the hand and swinging its body around in a circular or cranking motion until the head is separated.
> "Ketch me a couple of them fryin'-sized roosters an' ring their necks, 'cause we're gonna git company today."

RISIN'
A boil.
> "I guess Thelbert's blood is bad 'cause he's allus a-gittin' a risin'."

RIT
1. Dye, derived from the brand name of a fabric dye.
> "Gertrude, if you'd take an' Rit that dress a bright blue it shore would be perty."

2. Written, wrote.
> "Mavis rit her man a letter tryin' to get him to send somethin' back home fer the young-uns but he ain't sent nothin' an' he ain't rit her back neither."

RIVE
Split or divide into pieces.
> "Grandpa use to take his maul an' froe an' rive roof shingles an' fence palin's fer ever'body in this part of the country."

RIZ
Rose.
"Two hours after the sun riz it was hot enough to fry a egg on a rock."

Overheard . . .
"Bobby Lee's got perty good sense, but he cuts the fool so much you kain't tell it."

ROCK HIM BACK HOME
To throw rocks at an animal as a means of chasing him back home.
"If Old Bruno ever wanders over to your house, jist rock him back home."

ROOT, HOG, OR DIE
An expression meaning that one must take care of his own problems.
"Their Paw died when them young-uns was little, an' right quick they found that it had to be root, hog, or die."

ROUGH AS A COB
Severe, harsh, difficult.
"When you're the oldest boy with no daddy around, it can be rough as a cob."

ROUGH or TOUGH CUSTOMER
Mean, dangerous.
"Folks say it don't pay to tangle with the new shurf, 'cause he's one more rough customer."

ROUNDER
One who lacks restraint or has loose morals.
"W.G. shore was a rounder till Mabel got a-holt of him an' tuck him to the preacher fer one of them 'I do' parties."

ROUSE THEM UP
Awaken them.
"Hit's nearly five o'clock an' them young-uns still ain't stirrin'. Better rouse them up 'cause I'm fixin' to put the biscuits on the table."

RUN AWAY
Elope.
"Z.P. an' Doris had to run away to git married 'cause Doris' daddy was a sharecropper an' Z.P's daddy owned the farm an' wasn't about to approve of no marriage to no low-livin' sharecropper's daughter."

RUN DOWN
1. Weak, lacking energy.
"I ain't never got over that bad spell of flu—been run down ever since."
2. Criticize.
"I thank if a body don't do nothin' but run down somebody all the time, they ain't never gonna do no better."

RUN OVER
Mistreat.
"I despise to see them big old young-uns run over the little-uns."

RUN THANGS INTO THE GROUND
Overdone actions or words.
"Melvin goes around pullin' stunts on folks so much they're about tard of it. He jist likes to run thangs into the ground."

RUN THROUGH WITH
Squander, waste.
"His daddy left him a bunch of money but he run through with it an' didn't have a thang to show fer it."

RUN TOGETHER
What friends of the same sex who go places together do.
"Me an' Dora Mae run together till she up an' got hitched to my feller."

RUN YOU WILD
Drive you out of your mind.
"Looks like to me that havin' eight head of young-uns a-hollerin' an' screamin' all the time'd jist about run you wild."

RURN, RURNT
Ruin, ruined.
"Hobert, you're gonna rurn that dog if you don't make him mind . . . if he ain't done been rurnt already."

◄ S ►

SACK
Bag.
"Ain't no use to drag that cotton sack an' wear it out when it's empty. Pick it up an' tote it till you start pickin'."

SALLET
Salad, as in turnip or poke sallet.
"Some folks say poke sallet tastes a lot like spinach, but I don't know; I ain't never eat no spinach."

SANG
1. Sing.
"Charlie use to sang bass pertier than anybody I ever heered."
2. Ginseng.
"Clivas use to make right good money diggin' sang but it's jist about run out. Now he jist digs ramps."

SARTIN
Certain.
"I ain't plumb sartin, but I thank sprang water is a heap better than well water."

SASS
To speak impudently.
"I ain't gonna have no young-un of mine to sass me."

SAWED-OFF
Short in stature.
"Can you imagine Dora Lynn, the pertiest girl in the county, a-pickin' that little sawed-off funny-talkin' smart aleck to git married to?"

SAWMILL GRAVY *see* HOOVER GRAVY

SAY
Pronounce.
"How do you say that feller's name that's the new teacher?"

SCARCE AS HEN'S TEETH
Very scarce, since a hen has no teeth.
"If a body hadn't raised the stuff he et, I reckin he'd uv starved, 'cause money was scarce as hen's teeth back then."

SAUCERED AND BLOWED

When a coffee-drinking gentleman is seated next to a lady who is also drinking coffee, he has been known to offer, "Take mine, ma'am, it's done been saucered and blowed."

First a portion of hot liquid, usually coffee, is poured from a cup into a saucer. The saucered liquid has a greater surface area and it's shallower, which causes faster cooling. Blowing one's breath across the liquid further hastens cooling. Now it's probably cool enough to drink—from the saucer. Also, when drinking from the saucer, even further cooling can be affected by not letting the saucer quite touch the lips so the coffee has to be sucked that short distance through the air. It's a little noisy but effective.

SCARED MY MULE
Frightened me.
"I ain't never seen nothin' that scared my mule more'n one of them toynaders, an' I don't never want to see another'n."

SCOOTERPOOPIN'
Partying.
"Ever Saturday night me an' old J.C.'d go scooterpoopin'. Most generally we'd end up at that jook joint down at the county line."

SCOTCH
To block with a chock to prevent rolling.
"Uncle Lee use to scotch one of the hind wheels on his Model T, jack up the other'n, put er in high, an' twist the crank till it fired off. That jacked-up wheel would jist be a-spinnin' till he threwed it out of gear."

SCRAWNY
Gaunt and bony.

"Shorty said he didn't want no scrawny gal fer no wife—no less than 200 pounds with her shoes off an' her feet washed. Said he wanted one big enough to keep him warm in the winter an' shade him in the summer."

SCROOCH
Cuddle, snuggle.

"Scrooch up here close to me an' I'll put my coat around you."

SCROWGE
Press, crowd.

"Many's the time when they use to scrowge six of us young-uns on a pallet, feet-to-feet."

SCRUMPTIOUS
Delightful, excellent, delicious.

"I druther have a bunch of vegetables right out of the garden than any kind of meat. Now they're somethin' scrumptious."

SCRUNCH
Crunch, crush.

"Whenever Percy starts to scrunch on somethin' like a carrot or a cabbage core you can hear him across a 10-acre field."

SECOND TABLE
When there are not enough places at the table for everyone to eat together, a second table is served after the first have finished eating.

"Hit ain't no fair makin' us young-uns wait fer second table 'cause we don't hardly ever git no cake ner pie, an' we jist git wangs, backs, necks, an' feet."

SEE AFTER
Care for.

"Aint Carrie lives way off down in that holler by herself without a soul in the world to see after her."

SEED
Saw.

"Take your hands off of that-there gal! I seed her first."

SELLIN' OUT
Moving at a rapid pace.
"Last time I seen Luke he was in his old Ford headin' south on the hard road, sellin' out."

SET HIS CAP FOR
To be attracted to a girl and start making plans for getting to know her.
"I don't reckin Charlene knows about it, but Doug has done set his cap for her."

SET IN
Begin or began.
"When it finally set in to rainin', hit come a toad-strangler."

SETTIN' OF EGGS
Eggs, normally twelve to fifteen, placed under a hen to be hatched.
"I ain't had no rooster old enough to do my hens any good, so I'd like to swap you a settin' of eggs 'cause you've got some fine roosters."

SET UP WITH
A vigil, especially staying awake all night to minister to a person who is dangerously ill.
"Barney is so bad off that some of us has been takin' time about so we can set up with him all night, sort of in shifts, you might say."

SHADE-TREE MECHANIC
A mechanic with limited skills and training.
"I ain't a-trustin' my new Ford to no shade-tree mechanic."

SHADER
Shadow.
"A shader is a big thang of a mornin' but keeps gittin' littler, an' by dinner a body can jist about stand on the whole thang."

SHALLER
Shallow.
"They've jist got a shaller well an' it's mighty close to the barn. I'd be skeered of it if it was me."

SHANK OF THE EVENING
Late afternoon.
> "We never got back from the baptizin' till along about the shank of the evening."

SHED
Rid, discard.
> "Know anybody that's got a good rabbit dog they want to git shed of?"

SHELL OUT
Hand over, pay.
> "Whoever comes along that's ready to shell out my price, in cash, can have that mare mule."

SHENANIGAN
A devious trick, questionable practice, or conduct.
> "Hank is still pullin' off some kind of shenanigan jist like when he was a young-un."

SHET
Shut, close.
> "I shet my doors at night but leave the winders open."

SHIRT-TAIL BOY
A young boy, usually under twelve, derived from the fact that in some areas younger boys wore long shirts instead of pants.
> "Wayford, I've knowed your daddy ever since he was a shirt-tail boy, an' I allus thought a lot of him."

SHOE-MOUTH DEEP
Shoe-top deep.
> "In March, it come a snow about shoe-mouth deep."

SHOESTRING
1. Shoelace.
> "When I first heard somebody talkin' about a shoelace I thought it was some kind of fancy lace, not a shoestring."

2. A small amount of money.
> "He started on a shoestring and worked up . . . but she stopped him at the knee. He must have misunderstood about startin' on a shoestring."

SHORE
Sure.
"It don't make no sense fer it to be sitch a crime to be caught with a bottle of whiskey in a dry county but it ain't hardly nothin' to be caught drunk."

SHORE-NUFF
Real.
"Mamma lets me smoke rabbit tobacker but if she ever caught me smokin' shore-nuff tobacker she'd give me a good stripin'."

SHOT MY WAD
Finished, energy used up.
"By nine o'clock of a evenin' I've done shot my wad."

SHOT UP
Grew exceptionally fast.
"That little old wormy boy of the Benson's has done shot up to whir he's as big as a grown man."

SHOWED HER MY HEELS
Left her.
"When Audry started tellin' me about what a big weddin' her mamma planned on havin' fer us an' I hadn't said nothin' about marryin', I got scared an' showed her my heels."

SHOWIN' OUT
Showing off.
"Bert was jist showin' out, tryin' to impress them girls."

SHUCK
1. Shook.
"Hit come a big clap of thunder that near bout shuck the pitchers off of the wall."
2. Husk.
"Ezrey, when you shuck that corn save me some shucks fer my cow."
3. Remove.
"We use to go down to the swimmin' hole in the creek an' jist shuck off our duds an' jump in jaybird. Never even heard tell of a bathin' suit."

SHURF
Sheriff.
> "The high shurf is the onliest one that has to git elected. Then he hires all the deputies hisself."

SHUT YOUR MOUTH
Quit talking.
> "Shut your mouth, young-un, grown folks is a-talkin'."

SIC UM
A hunter's cry to his dogs to seek, chase, or attack something.
> "Whenever I holler to old Vise Jaw to 'sic um,' they ain't a hog in the woods that he kain't ketch."

Overheard . . .
"Ma's as busy as a three-legged cat under a guava tree today."

SIDE WITH
Defend, join.
> "When a man an' his wife is fightin', you better not side with either one of um er they'll both jump on you."

SIGHT UNSEEN
Without looking.
> "Shorty, I'll swap knives with you sight unseen."

SIGNS
The twelve signs of the zodiac.
> "If a body don't plant by the signs, stuff won't never make as good as when he does. You have to plant thangs that grows above the ground on the light of the moon an' stuff that grows below the ground, durin' the dark of the moon."

SILENTS
Motion pictures without sound.
> "They generally hard a feller to play a piano to make them silents more excitin'."

SINK OR SWIM
An expression meaning do for yourself or do without.
"Edgar jist flat out told his boy that if he left home to not come crawlin' back. He'd have to sink or swim."

SIRP
Syrup, when made from maple or cane, but not sorghum—that's molasses.
"Mamma use to fix sugar sirp, jist sugar an' water, an' it looked and tasted like white Karo to me."

SITCH
Such.
"Bobby said I was the one that told on him, but I never done no sitch a thang."

SKEETER
1. Mosquito.
"I like to go out campin' early in the sprang when you ain't as likely to git bit by a skeeter."
2. A small car with all, or most all, of its body removed.
"Nugene tuck an' stripped ever'thang that wasn't needed off of his flivver an' made a skeeter out of it."

SKINT
Skinned.
"I skint my foot so bad I kain't wear a slipper on it."

SKITTISH
Easily frightened.
"Bufford shore got helt up when he traded fer that old skittish horse. He's allus seein' boogers an' he's done throwed Bufford twict."

SLAM
Totally, all the way.
"It took eight gallons to fill the tank slam full."

SLAP
Completely.
"I kain't bake no biscuits this mornin'; I'm slap out of flour."

SLAUNCHWAYS
Skewed, slanted, crosswise, not straight.
"Don is so tall he has to lay slaunchways on a reg'ler bed."

SLEW
A large number.
"My taters made good. I mean I got a slew of um this year."

Overheard . . .
"You ain't foolin' me—mamma didn't raise no idiots."

SLIPPER SPOON
Shoe horn.
"Looks like my feet has swole er spread out from goin' barefooted. See if you can find that slipper spoon fer me."

SLOSH
Splash.
"Walter, you better put a tater on the spout of that coal oil can so it won't slosh out in the wagon an' git on the eatin' stuff."

SLOW HURRY
A mild rush, no need to get into a sweat about it.
"I'm sort of in a slow hurry now, but I'll stop by later on this evenin'."

SLOW TIME
Central time; Eastern time is fast.
"Down in Floridy they've got fast time but I druther have slow time."

SMACK
1. To open and close the lips noisily, especially while eating.
"Karl said he jist had to smack his lips real loud 'cause the food was so good."
2. An open-handed blow or slap to the face.
"It's easy to shore-nuff hurt a young-un if you smack um. Nature provided a better place."
3. A kiss.
"Berline didn't jist give me a smack on the jaw; it was a shore-nuff kiss."

SMACK-DAB
Exactly, squarely.
"They live smack-dab in the middle of nowheres."

SMELLS LOUD
A strong fragrance or odor.
"Check fer a rotten tater in that sack. Somethin' shore smells loud."

SMELT
Smelled.
"That polecat sprayed old Rover an' we smelt him fer three days."

SMIDGEN
A small amount.
"It'd be a heap better with jist a smidgen more salt."

SNAKE DOCTOR
Dragon fly, mosquito hawk.
"They has to be a sick snake around here sommers. See if you can kill that devilish snake doctor 'fore it cures him."

SNAKE LOGS
To move logs by dragging.
"It's easier to snake logs up in the yard to cut farr wood than to cut it in the woods an' have to haul it."

SMART PILLS

One feller told another'n one time that he had some real special pills that would make anybody smart as a whip if he took um fer a few days. The second feller was all fer tryin' um an' took about a dozen home with him. After he had took nearly all of um, he run up on the one he got um from an' said to him, "I don't thank these-here smart pills is worth a hill of beans. They look jist like rabbit pills an' I'm beginnin' to thank that's all they are."

"See there what I told you. You're done gittin' smart already!"

> ## SNIPE HUNT
>
> A snipe hunt was a prank pulled on someone uninitiated. The novice was taken out at night and posted in a ditch or gully where he was to hold open a sack pointed up the gully. All others left. They were to be rounding up snipes and driving them down the gully to be caught in the open sack held by the uninitiated person. The prank is that there are no snipes and the sack holder is left "holdin' the bag."

SNUCK
Sneaked.

"He nearly snuck right up on me from behind but I smelt his asifidity."

SODY
Soda.

"A body can use sody fer a lot more thangs than bakin'; it's good fer jist a whole heap of ailments. I reckin there must be sody in a strawberry sody water too."

SOMMERS
Somewhere.

"You kain't hardly ever ketch Vernon at home 'cause he's nearly allus gone sommers."

SOONER
Rather.

"I'd sooner do without no help than to have a hard hand that's a drunk."

SOPPIN' GRAVY
Gravy that is to be sopped with a piece of bread or biscuit.

"About six cathead biscuits an' a big plate of soppin' gravy ort to last me till dinner, I reckin."

SOPPIN' WET
Soaking wet.

"Arnold got soppin' wet jist comin' from the barn to the house."

SORE-HEADED
Disagreeable, ill-natured.
"A feller jist kain't please that old sore-headed teacher."

SORRY
Worthless, useless.
"A body kain't do much whittlin' with a old sorry knife."

SORTA
Sort of.
"It never made much diff'runce whir Donna was a-standin' er a-layin' she was still five foot high. I reckin you could call her sorta fat."

SOT
1. Sat.
"First one neighbor then the other'n sot up with Alice Marie till she pulled through her sickness."
2. A full-time drunkard.
"The main difference between a sot an' a alcoholic is that a sot don't have to go to all them meetin's."

SOW BELLY
Salt pork.
"You take an' fry sow belly good an' crisp an' hits better'n lean meat."

Overheard . . .
"Any time you pass my house I'd appreciate it."

SPARKIN'
Dating.
"Whenever I was sparkin' hit would take quite a spell 'fore I'd git up enough nerve jist to hold a girl's hand."

SPEAR
Superior.
"I jist don't see how anybody can figger they're spear to other folks jist 'cause they've got a lot of book learnin'. Shucks, while they was in school other folks was a-learnin' a lot of stuff, too."

SPECKS
Short for spectacles, eyeglasses.
"Ten year ago I could count the toes on a chigger. Now I kain't hardly see to git around without specks."

> *Overheard . . .*
> "I kain't say, 'cause I ain't no judge, an' there ain't enough of me to be no jury neither."

SPECK SO
Probably, very likely.
"Harry says Mabel is so perty some sorry old boy'll rurn her 'fore she's sixteen, an' I speck so myself."

SPIED
Saw.
"Guess who I spied down by the creek? It was Leona and that drummer all wrapped up in a blanket, and I needn't tell you the rest."

SPILL THE BEANS
To divulge a secret.
"Nobody'd ever found out if it hadn't been fer old blabbermouth Mabel; she jist had to go an' spill the beans."

SPISHYUS
Suspicious.
"I jist about knowed that them fellers was the ones that had robbed the store. They looked might spishyus to me first time I seen um."

SPITTIN' IMAGE
Exactly alike.
"They're the spittin' image of each other jist to look at um, but they ain't nothin' alike in the way they act."

SPITTIN' INTO THE WIND
A fruitless endeavor.
"Sam is so hardheaded that tryin' to tell him anythang is like spittin' into the wind."

SPOSE
Suppose, supposed.
"Do you spose that horse can ever be learnt to plow like he's spose to?"

SPRADDLE LEG-GED
A wide stance.
"A feller kain't keep his balance ridin' in a wagon standin' up 'less he stands spraddle leg-ged. Sailors tell me that's the way they ride on them boats too."

SPRANGS
Springs.
"Vernon's wagon had a seat with sprangs on it an' hit rode as good as a buggy."

SPRINGS

If folks was lucky enough to have a good sprang of water on their place, an' if it was right close to the house, they never had to dig no well. You could jist take a gourd dipper, er a store-bought one if you didn't have nairn, an' dip a fresh drank right out of the sprang and then fill your bucket if you brung one. If you was thirsty an' didn't have no dipper it was easy to jist scoop up a double handful of water an' drank right out of your hands. Young-uns liked to jist lay down on their bellies an' drank like a horse.

Because folks never had no ice box to keep thangs cool, they'd use the sprang fer that too. They'd put their milk in a sirp er lard bucket that had a tight-fittin' lid on it an' set it in the sprang. You had to put a rock un top of the bucket though, er it'd float away. When it come a hard rain an' the creek'd git up it'd drown out the sprang an' float the milk away if you didn't run down an' git it out. As long as the creek stayed up, there wouldn't be no drankin' water 'less you'd ketch some rainwater to hold you over.

SPRING CHICKEN
Young person.
"She shore ain't no spring chicken like she makes out like. She's forty-five if she's a day."

SQUINCH-EYED
Squint-eyed, cross-eyed.
"Whenever I git out in that bright sun it makes me squinch-eyed."

SQUIRTS
Diarrhea.
"Vernon ate somethin' that give him a real bad case of the squirts."

SQUZ
Squeezed.
"Mamma tuck an' squz three lemons in a bucket of water, put in a little sugar, an' we all had us some lemonade."

STAND GOOD FOR
Assume responsibility for another's obligation.
"I'll stand good for the boy to buy that car 'cause he kain't buy it without no credit."

STAND UP FOR
Act as a witness.
"Folks don't say 'stand up for' much no more. They say 'best man' instead."

STANG
Sting.
"The best thang a body can do fer a bee, wasp, er a yeller jacket stang is to hold a piece of ice on it. Chewed-up tobacker is about the next best thang."

STEEPLES
Staples.
"That old cow's been runnin' her head through the fence an' has jist about pushed out all of the steeples."

STEP OFF THE CARPET
Get married.
"Never thought Gertie would step off the carpet. I figgered she was havin' too much fun playin' the field."

STICK TO YOUR RIBS
Food that will provide long-lasting strength and energy.
"I've got to have me some beans an' taters fer dinner ever day—them's somethin' that'll stick to your ribs."

STIR AROUND
1. Move about.
"Thelma's out of bed an' able to stir around a little now."
2. Get a move on.
"Y'all better stir around if you don't want to be late fer Sunday school."

Overheard . . .
"In the wintertime the outhouse was too far away; in the summertime it was too close."

STOCK
1. Trust, faith, confidence.
"I don't take no stock in nobody that is allus blowin' off about what a good Christian he is."
2. Livestock.
"A body that's got chickens an' stock kain't never hardly git away fer long."

STOLD
Stole.
"Mr. Weathers has got piles of money all right an' I know whir he got the most of it—he stold it from his sharecroppers."

STOMPING GROUND
Favorite or home territory.
"I got so homesick I jist had to git back to my old stomping ground."

STORE-BOUGHT
Bought, as opposed to homemade.
"I liked them toys Uncle Doyce made fer me a whole heap better than store-bought ones."

STORY
Lie.
"If I said somebody told a story that's all right, but if I was to say they told a lie, I'd git a whuppin' fer sayin' it."

STOUT
Physically strong.
"Misseries Crowder is the kind of woman you don't want to tangle with 'cause she's as stout as a mule."

STOVE UP
Injured or crippled to such a degree that it is difficult or impossible to get around.
"Old man Morgan's boys cut his winter's wood fer him 'cause he's too stove up to do hardly anythang."

STRACK
Strike.
"A feller that'll strack a match to light a smoke a-settin' in front of a farr must have more money than sense."

STRANGS
Strings.
"Will can pick up anythang with strangs on it an' make music."

STRUCK ON
Infatuated by, or in love with, something or someone.
"J.T.'s struck on that new postmistress but she ain't got no idy that he is."

STUCK UP
Conceited, self-important.
" I kain't see, for the life of me, why Jim Bob an' Ailene is so stuck up. They don't own a thang in the world that's free an' clear."

STUMPED
1. Baffled.
"Why the Maker decided not to put no upper teeth in a cow has got me stumped."
2. Stubbed.
"I stumped my big toe an' knocked the hide off of it."

STUMP-FLOATER
A heavy rain, one that will cause flooding.
"When hit come that stump-floater Thursday was a week ago, half of my garden got washed away."

STUMP SPEECH
A public speech, usually political.
"Anytime a politician can gather a handful of people, you're gonna git a stump speech."

SUCKER
Lollipop.
"First time I heard somebody call a sucker a lollipop I never knowed what they was a-talkin' about."

SUCKIN' ON THE HIND TIT
Getting less than a fair share.
"I'm glad fer Melvin that he got that good job; he's been suckin' on the hind tit all his life."

SUGAR
A kiss.
"A feller that eats them ramps kain't expect to git no sugar fer a week."

SULL
Sulk; to curl up and lie still as if dead, the way possums do.
"I druther Wyvonna'd jist speak her mind to me when she gits mad, but all she'll do is sull, so I don't even know what she's mad about a lot of times."

SUMMERSET
Somersault.
"Regina never could learn to do a summerset."

SUNDAY-GO-TO-MEETIN' CLOTHES
Best clothes.
> "Herb must be runnin' fer somethin'. I seen him in town all dressed up in his Sunday-go-to-meetin' clothes."

SUN TO SUN
From sunup to sundown, the work day on a farm during hard times.
> "Mance use to work from sun to sun an' be up half the night daincin' and boozin'."

SUT
Soot.
> "Them boys would smoke anythang that would burn, like corn silks, grape vines, rabbit tobacker, catalpa beans, and even chimley sut."

SWALLER
Swallow, believe.
> "Hit's hard fer me to swaller all them tales that Z.P. tells about when he was in the army."

Overheard . . .
"We go to bed with the chickens an' git up with the rooster."

SWALLOW A PUNKIN' SEED
To become pregnant.
> "Erminee says she likes boys real good but is afraid if she likes them too good she might swallow a punkin' seed."

SWANG
Swing.
> "Bow to your partner an' give her a swang, then promenade her 'round the rang. With the little foot up an' the big foot down, all promenade go 'round the town."

SWAP SLOBBERS
Kiss.
> "Nadine won't drink out of the same dipper that somebody else has drunk out of, but she'll swap slobbers with any boy in school."

SWOLE
Swollen.
"A swole belly ain't allus from eatin' too many taters."

> *Overheard . . .*
> "Fireball Wilson's so slow it wouldn't hurt him none to fall out of a tree."

◄ T ►

TACKY
Unfashionable, shabby.
"Marge wore tacky clothes all right, but she allus washed her neck an' ears good."

TAD
A small or insignificant amount or degree, bit.
"I ain't complainin', you understand, but I thank them beans need a tad more salt."

TAGS OF ICE
Icicles.
"It rained an' turned cold durin' the night an' tags of ice was hangin' from the eaves all around the house."

TAKE DINNER WITH US
An invitation to stay and eat the noon meal.
"Y'all don't be in no rush. You're welcome to jist stay an' take dinner with us."

TAKE IN
1. Begin, as when school or church starts.
"The school bus didn't hardly ever git to the school before it was time to take in, but the teacher never did mark us tardy, 'cause we couldn't help it."
2. Attend, enjoy.
"All of us is goin' to take in the fair."

Overheard . . .
"I'd rather shake than rattle." (Spoken by a heavy, plump woman.)

TAKEN
Took.
"Butch taken a likin' to his teacher the first day."

TAKEN or TOOK A SHINE TO
Favorably impressed, found desirable.
"Looks like Dr. Walker has taken a shine to the new schoolmarm, don't it?"

Overheard . . .
"Bill Townsend's racehorse was sort of slow-footed."

TAKE ON
Make a big fuss over, or to grieve.
"When a person will take on like Marie did when her little dog died, I don't see how she could stand it if Leroy died."

TAKE OUT
1. To unhitch an animal.
"When that dinner bell rings old Laura wants to head fer the barn, so I might jist as well take out."
2. To set out or go.
"Jist after dinner on Saturday, Daddy'd allus take out fer town."

TAKE PAINS
To put in as much time and effort as needed to do something well.
"Them women was surprised that Ed made that quilt. He shore takes pains an' it shows."

TAKES AFTER
Has similar looks or traits.
"There ain't a one of them Roberson young-uns that takes after their mamma; they're all the spittin' image of Rex."

TAKE TIME ABOUT
Take turns.
"Don't y'all big young-uns hog the swang. Take time about with the littler ones."

TAKE UP BOOKS
A call to lessons.
"When Miss Miller rangs her bell, that means it's time to take up books."

TAKING IN
Attending.
> "Next week ever last one of us is gonna be taking in the fair."

TALKIN' UP A BLUE STREAK
Prolonged fast talking.
> "That salesman was talkin' up a blue streak tryin' to sell a vacuum cleaner to Kate an' didn't never give her time to tell him she didn't have no 'lectric."

TALK UGLY
Use vulgar language.
> "Robert Ed has got a mighty nasty mouth, but I can say one thang fer him, he don't never talk ugly in front of womenfolks ner young-uns."

TALK UP A STORM
Talk a lot and then some.
> "Clarence don't never talk much 'less it's about football, an' then he'll talk up a storm."

TALLYWHACKER
Penis.
> "When Henry was four year old he was a-settin' on the ground wearin' them little short pants an' his little tallywhacker fell out of the peein' slot. One of them big old ganders spied it an' must uv thought it was a worm an' grabbed it, an' before they could shoo him off, the pore little feller was durn near rurnt."

TALL TALES

Humor often took the form of tall tales, such as this yarn:

"We git a awful lot of our table food thisaway. You take a 'possum er somethin' that's been run over a lot on the road an' mashed flat as a flitter, an' you can scoop that sucker up, take him home an' soak him fer three er four hours an' he'll swell right back up again."

TANKED UP
Inebriated, intoxicated, drunk.
"Pete don't git tanked up very often, but when he does he might be on one fer a week."

TAR
Tire for a vehicle.
"We never had no jack in the car so Lester jist cut a saplin' to use fer a prize pole when we had that flat tar."

TARD
Tired.
"I git tard of eatin' biscuits an' corn bread all the time. Wunct in a while I'd like to have me a whole loaf of light bread to eat all at one time."

TASTE OF IT
Taste it.
"Taste of it an' see how you like it."

TATER
Potato.
"I can make a meal anytime out of a bowl of beans, a tater, a hunk of corn bread, an' a glass of buttermilk."

TEA CAKE
Any of various cookies.
"A tea cake use to be the fanciest kind of sweet stuff we ever got."

TELL ON
1. Tattle.
"You better quit messin' up my playhouse er I'm gonna tell on you."
2. Take its toll.
"Workin' in the field an' havin' a houseful of chillern to raise is beginnin' to tell on pore old Misseries Blankenship. She's broke a lot this past year."

TENDIN' LAND
Cultivating land or farming, usually for someone else.
"The only thang Dayton knows is tendin' land and he won't try to learn nothin' else."

TENANT FARMING

Tenant farmers worked fer the other feller an' paid him fer the use of the land an' a shack to live in. The landlord collected a part of the "cash" crop, usually tobacker er cotton, an' a part of the corn.

'Cause I jist know first hand about cotton and corn farmin', I'll stick to that.*

There was two kinds of tenant farmers: renters an' sharecroppers. Renters had their own horse er mule an' their own plows, cultivators, planters, fertilizers, an' a wagon. They paid the landlord a third of the corn an' a fourth of the cotton, er what folks called it "farmin' on a third an' fourth." They was "supposed to get" half of the cotton an' half of the corn at gatherin' time. A sharecropper didn't have nothin' but his back an' hands, his wife's, an' his young-uns's.

Most of the time the landlord owned a store too, er made 'rangements with somebody that did, an' he would "carry" er "furnish" the sharecropper until fall. The landlord kept the book an' done all the figgerin'. A lot of them farmers never knowed how to read nor write anyhow. Some sharecroppers was white, some was black, an' ever'-body got the same deal.

A average size farm was maybe forty acres. Gardens, chickens, an' a hog er two was mostly what they had to eat on. Neighbors with cows would usually divide their buttermilk an' clabber.

Schools would let out durin' cotton pickin' time so the young-uns could help pick cotton. Gatherin' time an' Christmas was what ever'body looked forward to all year, 'cause then they'd git some money. In many, maybe I should say most, cases, it jist didn't work out that way. The sharecropper's half usually wouldn't even pay off what was on the book at the store, according to the storekeeper's figures. Of course it was slavery . . . but it was legal.

*The author became a sharecropper at twelve years of age.

TETCHED
Mentally deficient.
"Ever since that mule kicked Thelbert up side of the head he's been a little tetched, pore feller."

THANG
Thing.
"One thang I know is thangs is never the same the second time around."

THANK
Think.
"With all the noise in that mill I don't see how them folks that works thar can even thank."

THAR
There.
"When the roll is called up yonder, I'll be thar."

THATAWAY
That direction.
"Sheriff, them varmints went thataway, torge Buzzard Gulch."

THAT-THERE
That.
"What do you reckin that-there watermelon would weigh?"

THAY
There.
"Thay jist wasn't nobody that could daince the Charleston better'n Nadine."

THEIRN
Theirs.
"Ever'thang of theirn is bought an' paid fer."

THEIRSELVES
Themselves.
"Don's an' Betty's folks never give them nothin'. What they've got they made it all by theirselves."

THEM
Those.
"What do you git fer them brogan shoes?"

THESE-HERE
These.
"Mamma-she had eight head of young-uns an' these-here are three of my brothers: Tom, Nick, an' Larry."

Overheard . . .
"Ever'body that was within the sound of the bell's voice come a-runnin'."

THINGAMAJIG
Something that is hard to classify or whose name is unknown or forgotten.
"Aubry's new Model A has a thingamajig that shows how many miles a hour a feller is goin', but most of the time he don't ride fer a hour anyway so it won't do him much good."

THINK HARD OF
Get mad at.
"Tonnis was allus a-gittin' drunk an' gittin' throwed in the calaboose, but he never harmed nobody an' folks didn't never think hard of him fer it."

THIS-HERE
This.
"How'd you like to swap your gun fer this-here fine huntin' dawg of mine?"

THOAT
Throat.
"I've had a cold an' sore thoat since Christmas."

THOB
Throb.
"My mashed fanger didn't do nothin' but thob all night."

THOUGHT THE WORLD OF
Had very high regard for.
"I allus figgered Bob and Grace thought the world of each other, but first thang you knowed they had parted."

THOW
Throw.
"Thow me one of them apples while you're up the tree."

THRASH
Beat, whip.
"The principal use to thrash whoever needed it—even football players."

THREE SHEETS TO THE WIND
Drunk.
"Clyde allus gits three sheets to the wind ever payday."

THROW A LITTLE AIR IN THEM TARS
Inflate the tires.
"Better throw a little air in them tars 'fore you head out. They all look a little slack to me."

THROWED
Threw.
"Percy throwed ball awhile in the minor leagues."

THROWED IT DOWN
Gave it up.
"I use to be the biggest drunkard there ever was, but I throwed it down."

Overheard . . .
"I'll be ready when the Big Mornin' comes."

THROW IT UP TO
A reminder or rehash of a mistake or something unpleasant.
"You don't have to throw it up to me about what I done. I've mended my ways, so let it be."

THROW OFF ON
Criticize, belittle.
"If folks wouldn't allus throw off on Luke all the time he might have the heart to do better."

THU
Through.
"By the time I git thu with one thang there's three more jobs done stacked up on me."

THUNK
Thought.
"The skunk thunk the stump stunk, but the stump thunk the skunk stunk."

Overheard . . .
"Dewey weighed 150 pounds with his britches off and his feet washed."

TIED DOWN
Obligated; being married, especially with children.
"Hit don't seem to make no nevermind that Melvin's got a wife an' young-uns. He's allus out boozin' an' chasin' skirts anyhow . . . kain't stand bein' tied down."

TOAD- or FROG-STRANGLER
A very hard rain.
"It come a toad-strangler last night an' the creek by the barn is still too high to ford."

TOBACKER or BACKER
Tobacco.
"Wouldn't it have been somethin' to be around the first time somebody dipped er chewed er smoked tobacker?"

TOLABLE
Tolerable, fairly satisfactory.
"Old man Varnell allus says he's tolable when you ask him how he is."

TOM WALKERS
Stilts.
> "First pair of Tom Walkers I ever had was made out of forked sticks."

TO MY KNOWIN'
To the best of my knowledge, as far as I know.
> "To my knowin' Jake's done had about a dozen young-uns by outside women."

TONGUE-TIED
Shy, speechless.
> "Harold allus gits tongue-tied when he gits around girls."

TOO BOWLEGGED TO HEM UP A SHOAT
An expression describing legs bowed to such an extent that a young hog could pass between them.
> "Larkin is too bowlegged to hem up a shoat. Why, if his legs was straightened out he'd be a head taller."

TOOK A FIT OVER
Liked a lot.
> "Them that tried Pauline's pie jist took a fit over it. They called it rhubarb, but I never heered tell of it bein' called anythang but pie plant before."

TOOK A NOTION
Decided.
> "When Helen took a notion to be a nurse, she stuck it out till she done it."

TOOK TO HER BED
Became bedfast.
> "When Lizzie's man, Aubry, died, she took to her bed on the day he was buried an' never got out of it. She jist lasted nine days from grievin'."

TOOK UP WITH
Assumed a close relationship.
> "They wasn't never married, they jist took up with each other."

TOOT
Valueless.
"I druther have my old knife back that I lost than this-here new one; it ain't worth a toot."

TOO WET TO PLOW
An expression meaning too bad or too late, derived from soil that is untillable because it is like mud.
"If I ever ketch you makin' eyes at another woman, it will be jist too wet to plow."

TORGE
Toward.
"We never got home till along torge dark-thirty."

TOSSEL
Tassel.
"My corn's done higher'n your head an' startin' to tossel."

TOTE
Carry.
"We had to tote all of our water clear up that steep hill."

T'OTHER
The other.
"I had to walk clear to town. They wasn't but two cars come by an' they was both a-headin' t'other way."

TOUCHOUS
Sore to the touch.
"That old sore on my arm is as touchous as a risin'."

TOUSLED
Rumpled, tangled mass, as of hair.
"I saw a pitcher of that feller Einstein. He's s'posed to be right smart, but his hair's so tousled he must not know much about hair combin'."

TOW SACK
Sack made of tow, gunny, or burlap.
"Mr. Wallace give me a tow sack full of taters fer helping him dig his."

TOYNADER
Tornado.
"I'm a heap more scared of a toynader than I am a hurricane 'cause there ain't no way of knowin' whir one's a-gonna hit."

TRADE HOWDIES
To exchange greetings.
"Them town folks ain't very sociable. When you try to trade howdies with them they jist look at you plumb quare."

TRAIPSE
Walk, wander.
"Charlie would jist as soon traipse around in the rain er snow as when the sun was shinin'. Made no nevermind to him."

TRAP DOOR
The buttoned flap in the seat of long underwear.
"I don't like them trap door long handles as good as them that you jist spread apart when you squat down. They are a heap quicker."

TRASHY
Low class.
"Ever'body says them Hendersons down on the branch is trashy, but I thank it's mostly 'cause they don't keep too clean an' Toby has let his hair grow out till it's nearly down to his collar. I guess they're perty good people though."

TRIFLIN'
Lazy, shiftless.
"Lonzo is so triflin' he won't button but one er two buttons on his shirt, leaves one of his gallowses off, an' won't never tie his brogans."

TROTS
Diarrhea.
"Pat had the trots so bad he had to keep runnin' to the woods all day."

TRUCK PATCH
A large vegetable garden usually grown for home use and marketing.
"If a body lives on a main road, he can generally do pretty good with a truck patch."

TRANSPORTATION

Most folks went afoot most ever'whir they wanted to go lessen it was a mighty fer piece. Folks that was well off had nice buggies an' horses but pore folks done good to have a mule an' wagon. If a body had a mule er a horse to ride they wouldn't usually have no saddle though. They'd jist throw a tow sack over its back an' climb on. If a whole bunch was goin' to a revival er somethin' they'd cover the wagon bed with straw er hay to set down er lay down on. A few folks had sprang seats that set on top of the wagon bed. Law, they rode nearly as good as a buggy.

'Fore long even pore folks started gittin' hold uv secondhand cars, mostly Model T Fords, an' fore long they got jist about as thick as buggies an' wagons. The cheapest ones was open, 'cept fer curtains. In rainy er cold weather them closed in ones with glass winders was mighty fine. Henry Ford sure made a whole mess of um them thangs from 1908 to 1927, but durin' Hoover days most folks jist had to set um up 'cause they jist couldn't buy gas an' tags fer um.

Nearly ever'body, 'cept share croppers, had a horse er a mule, an' somebody come up with a good idy fer usin' them Ts. They took off the front axle, wheels an' sprang an' made a two-wheel cart out of it that could be pulled by a horse er a mule. They never rurnt the T; they could jist put the stuff back when times got better. Some called um a "go cart" but most folks called um "Hoover carts."

TUCK
Took.

"One day Gladys jist up an' left, tuck the young-uns an' ever'thang, without so much as a howdy-do."

TUCKERED OUT
Exhausted.

"Maureen, honey, run to the sprang an' git me a cold bucket of water 'cause I don't thank I can make it. I'm plumb tuckered out."

TURN
1. A load, a quantity, an armful.
"When you take a turn of corn to the gristmill, the miller keeps a fourth of the meal for grindin' it."
2. Personality, outlook.
"Joan'll git along all right; she's got a good turn."

TURN A HAND
Work, make an effort.
"That sorry Geneva don't never turn a hand to help her pore old mamma do nothin'."

TURN LAND
To plow soil with a deep-cutting disk or winged turning plow.
"In the sprang when you turn land it shore does have a good smell to it."

TURN LOOSE SOME MONEY
Spend some money on goods or services.
"Them fellers at the fair are doin' their level best to git folks to turn loose some money, an' a lot of um do."

TURN OF THE SUN
Twelve o'clock noon.
"By the turn of the sun ever day I'm huntin' me some dinner."

TURN or RETURN THANKS
Say grace before eating.
"When the preacher'd come to eat fried chicken on Sunday, he'd turn thanks. I was little an' thought he was talkin' to the table."

TURTLE HULL
The trunk of a car.
"They're startin' to make cars now that's got a turtle hull built on them fer puttin' suitcases an' stuff in."

TWICT
Twice.
"Cut that out right now. An' I ain't gonna tell you twict!"

◄ U - V ►

UM
Them.

"Derene an' the young-uns is down at the bus station, an' I've got to go down an' pick um up."

UNBEKNOWNST
Happening without one's knowledge.

"Harry drawed out all of the money they had, unbeknownst to Alice, an' blowed it all."

UNLESSEN
Unless.

"We kain't git to the revival this week unlessen Geneva gits over the epizootics in time."

UP AGAINST IT
Having a difficult time.

"Since the mill shet down ever'body's jist been up against it."

UP AN' DIED
Expired.

"I seen Sammy last Thursday an' he seemed to be doin' extry good, then Sunday mornin' he jist up an' died."

UPPITY
Arrogant, putting on airs of superiority.

"Since Donna Sue's husband got to be foreman, she's so uppity her feet don't hardly hit the ground."

UP TO SNUFF
An expression having about the same meaning as "up to par."

"If ever'thang ain't up to snuff, Leroy won't let it go through."

USED TO COULD
Was once able to.

"I used to could work hard from sun to sun but now I give out 'fore dinner."

UV
Contraction for *have* as part of a verb.
"I could uv got done by dinner but a trace chain broke an' I had to find some balin' warr to fix it with."

VARMINT
A contemptible person, a rascal.
"Charlene spent enough time with that sorry varmint fer him to change if he was a-goin' to, but he never."

'VENCHLY
Eventually.
"There wasn't nobody that had a telephone but Miz Wallace way back then, but 'venchly jist about ever'body got one."

VITTLES

Gardens, chickens, an' a hog er two was mostly what folks had to eat on. Them that had cows would usually divide their buttermilk an' clabber with their neighbors.

Some good breakfasts was thick'nin' (Hoover) soppin' gravy an' biscuits; chicken, rabbit, partridge er squirrel fried in gravy; sirp er sorghum molasses an' hot biscuits. Them last two was good to use fer sugar too. They're called long sweet'nin'.

A lot of times fer supper folks'd jist have milk an' bread. The bread could be reg'ler corn bread, cracklin' kind, er a hoecake. The milk could be clabber, buttermilk, er sweet, accordin' to what was on hand.

If you had um, biled new potatoes along with English peas made a mighty good combination. Nearly ever'thang, like any kind of bean er pea, fresh er dried, had to have a chunk of pork meat fer seasonin'.

Pore folks'd eat whatever they had. If young-uns complained about what there was to eat, the mamma'd say, "Well, maybe you'll like what we have tomorrow er the next day . . . if we have anythang."

◄ W ►

WAGON GREASIN'
A measure of distance.

"Hit's a wagon greasin', a half-a-day's walkin', an' a hour of swangin' on a grapevine to git to Calvin's place."

WAIL
Well.

"Wail, I reckin I better git me a good water witch in here to show me whir I ort to dig my wail."

WAITIN' ON
Ministering to.

"Charice is a mighty fine woman. She was waitin' on her pore mamma night an' day all them years till the Lord finally took her to her reward."

WALK IN HIGH COTTON
To be prosperous or in good social standing.

"Since Ralph got that good job with the county, he's drivin' a big car an' walkin' in high cotton."

WALKIN' ON AIR
On cloud nine, ecstatic.

"High-pockets has done got to be a grandpa, an' he's walkin' on air."

WALKIN' THE STRAIGHT AND NARROW
Doing no wrong, abiding by the Good Book.

"From now on I'm walkin' the straight and narrow. The onliest way they'll git me back in the lock-up will be fer sangin' too loud in church."

WANGS
Wings.

"I hear tell that when them airplane drivers fly over you an' wiggle their wangs they're sayin' 'howdy' to you."

WARR
Wire.

"Some of these days maybe Clem'll put me a warr fence around my garden like he said he would three year ago."

WARSH
Wash.
"If the weather is fitten, womenfolks will usually warsh clothes on Monday an' do their arnin' on Tuesday."

WARSHIN'TON
Washington.
"I don't rightly know whir Warshin'ton is at, prob'ly way off up North sommers, but all I know is that they ain't nothin' but a bunch of idjuts that's a-runnin' thangs there."

WASN'T TURNED THAT WAY
Was not of that temperament, personality, or inclination.
"Durin' the war lots of women would run around on their men, but not Evelyn. She jist wasn't turned that way."

WAX
Chewing gum.
"Here's two pennies, an' I want me a stick of Juicy Fruit wax an' a stick of peppermint candy."

WAY BACK YONDER
A long time ago.
"Way back yonder young-uns didn't have much time to theirselves. They had to work right alongside of their mammas an' daddies in the fields jist to make a livin', and that's why they wasn't into as much mischief."

Overheard . . .
"A banker'll never drown in sweat."

WAY OFF
Far away.
"Even when them dogs is way off, you can tell which one is Mr. Eubanks' old Bugle Mouth."

WAY YONDER
Much, lots.
"Them ball players is a-wantin' a heap more money, an' they're already gittin' way yonder more than they ort to fer jist playin'."

WELLS

If there wasn't no close sprang, a body'd have to dig a well. First thang you'd have to do was find a dowser, somebody that knowed water witchin', to find out whir there was water. They can take a fork-ed stick, maybe from a peach tree, an' hold a fork in each hand plum level. Then they'd walk around whir you wanted a well, an' if there's water under the ground that stick'd start turnin' down so hard it'd jist about twist off the bark in the water witcher's hands. Them people's jist got a gift, I reckin.

Generally it won't be more'n 20 to 40 feet to water, an' you can git by with a dug well. Well diggers use real short-handled picks, matticks, an' shovels, an' they jist hunker down an' start diggin' a hole jist as little as they can fit into. Somebody on top draws out the dirt an' rocks a bucketful at a time till they hit water. The well digger digs out steps in the side.

If a well has to be deeper, they bring in a well drillin' machine an' bore a hole in the ground till they hit water. If it's six inches er bigger a long skinny bucket will go down in it, er most folks put in hand pumps. The usual bucket size fer either kind of well is ten quarts. They'll hang a pully over the well an' run a rope er chain over it an' hook it to the bucket. Some jist draw it out hand-over-hand, but it's a heap easier to crank it out with a windlass. You have to wire a weight to one side of the bucket to make it tilt an' sink so it'll fill up.

WELL FIXED
Has plenty of money.
"Emmet is well fixed, owns half of the county, jist about, an' he's got more money than God."

WELL OFF
Few problems or worries.
"Frank don't know yet how well off he is, gittin' shed of Trixie."

WENT THROUGH WITH EVER'THANG
Squandered his assets.

"Jim sold his fine place an' all of his stock when he got that good job at public works. Wellser, the job played out an' he started a-spendin' money like it was water . . . went through with ever'thang."

WERD
Word.

"I ain't got no idy how a body would say 'w-o-r-d' any kind of way but 'werd'. . . well, maybe 'wurd'."

WE-UNS
We all.

"Citified folks thank we-uns out here in the sticks is a little quare, but them's the ones that's quare, b'leeve you me."

WHAMMY or, stronger, DOUBLE WHAMMY
A magic curse or spell.

"Somethin's done put the double whammy on me, I reckin, 'cause I kain't hardly git out of one fix till I'm in another'n."

WHAT ALL
What.

"Clair, I'm takin' in Saturday evenin' in Rogersville. What all do you want me to brang you from King's Store?"

WHAT TIME IS IT BY YOUR WATCH AND CHAIN?
An expression used to ask the time.

"Seems like Emory's dinner bell ort to uv rung by now. What time is it by your watch and chain?"

WHEELBAR
Wheelbarrow; also called a Georgie (Georgia) buggy.

"If a feller's ever been in the army, he'll find out not to volunteer fer no truck drivin' job. Hit's pushin' a wheelbar; that's what it is."

WHERE ALL
Where collectively.

"Where all did y'all go on your trip?"

WHERE IN TARNATION
Where in the world.
"Where in tarnation is Warshin'ton anyhow? Likely it's a way up North."

WHETROCK
Whetstone used for sharpening tools.
"Bring me my whetrock down here to the hog pen. The moon's right fer cuttin' these pigs, an' I might as well git it done."

WHIPPERSNAPPER
A diminutive, insignificant, or presumptuous person.
"That second lieutenant, that young whippersnapper, is one of them 90-day wonders."

WHIR
1. Where.
"Whir can a feller git a job of work?"
2. Whether.
"I don't know whir I can stand eatin' corn bread fer breakfast much longer."

WHIR BOUTS
Where.
"I heered Mr. Williams needs some hoe hands. Do you know whir bouts he lives?"

WHO ALL
Who.
"Who all was at the square daince that I would uv knowed?"

WHOLE BUNCH
A lot, several, many.
"Warren throwed a stick of dynamite in the pond an' up come a whole bunch of fish, belly up."

WHOLE SHEBANG
All, everything.
"Sam went an' bought a house an' forty acres, mule, plow, tools, an' a wagon—the whole shebang."

WHOMPER-JAWED
Misshapen, misaligned, askew.
"That rail fence is all whomper-jawed. Looks terrible."

WHUP
Whip.
"Guess I'll have to give up coon huntin' on account of my emphysema. I kain't even whup a dog no more."

WHUPPED WITH A UGLY STICK
An expression explaining someone's being very ugly.
"She's a pretty good natured old gal, but she looks like she's been whupped with a ugly stick—more'n wunct."

WIDDER
Widow.
"Now that Henry has come into a little money, he'll have a time fightin' off all them widder women."

WIGGLE TAILS
Mosquito larvae.
"That rainwater out yonder in the tub's done got wiggle tails in it."

WINDER LIGHT
Window pane.
"Henry busted out that-there winder light shootin' his slingshot. He knowed he wasn't spose to shoot it torge the house ner nobody."

WISH BOOK
A mail order catalog.
"Jist got a new wish book so the old one can be took to the outhouse."

Overheard . . .
"A body shouldn't trust a tight-mouthed dog."

WONDER OUT LOUD
Think out loud before starting to think about anything in particular.
"No, I wasn't talkin' to myself, I was jist wonderin' out loud."

WON'T LAST TILL THE WATER GITS HOT
An expression meaning short-lived.
> "That little wormy feller is too light in the britches to handle that job. He won't last till the water gits hot."

WORMY
Small, skinny, runty.
> "I was in one of them health food places in the city, an' ever last one of them folks a-workin' in that store looked mighty wormy to me."

WORRIMENT
Trouble, worry.
> "Foolin' with them biddies shore is a lot of worriment, but I reckin it's worth a body's time in the long run if you pleasure in it."

WORSER
Worse.
> "Hit's a whole lot worser bad luck to break a lookin' glass than it is to have a black cat to cross your path. You can most generally go around the cat."

WOULDN'T HOLD A CANDLE TO
An expression meaning it can't compare.
> "Doctor Freeman's mighty good, but he wouldn't hold a candle to that new one, whatever his name is, that's jist started to practice here."

WOULDN'T PUT IT PAST HIM
An expression meaning one wouldn't be at all surprised.
> "If Lonnie gits a bellyful of Charlene, he jist might make tracks. I wouldn't put it past him."

WOUND UP
Finished.
> "Finally got my crops laid by—wound up in time to take in the big doin's on the Fourth."

WRONG SIDE OUTARDS
Wrong side out.
> "Clarence didn't light no light when he got up, an' he put his shirt on wrong side outards."

WUDNIT?
Wasn't it?

"It shore was a big shock to me when that little old Jersey had twin calves. Wudnit to you too?"

WUNCT
Once.

"I was standin' in this-here big bed of aints an' it looked like ever one of um took a notion to stang me all at wunct."

WUSH
Wish.

"I won't never forgit what a feller told me about gittin' somethin' by wushin' fer it. He said if you wush in one hand an' hockey in the other'n, see which one gits full first."

> *Overheard . . .*
> "My wife up an' left me, an' I don't miss her no more than a cold draft after the door's shet."

◄ X - Y - Z ►

Y'ALL
You all, all of you; never (correctly) used to address one person.
"Y'all might jist as well stay all night with us 'cause it'll be slap dark 'fore the creek goes down enough so you can ford it."

YALLER or YELLER
Yellow.
"Funny thang—them yaller-meated watermelons taste jist as red as the reg'ler kind."

YANKEE DIME
A kiss.
"Wanda Lou said she'd give me a dime to go to the sprang an' git her a fresh drank. All I got was a old yankee dime."

YEAH
Yes.
"Some children ain't very respectful. One boy in my class answered the teacher with a *yeah*, but she got him straight right quick—told him that in her class it would be *yes'um*."

YEAR
Ear.
"Old man Harris never did say *ear*, he allus said *year* fer ear."

YEP
Yes.
"Barney figured he'd git a yep out of Gertrude, but he got a nope."

YES'UM
Yes, ma'am.
"My boy is thirty years old but he still says 'yes'um' to me."

YISTIDDY
Yesterday.
"Eddy said the preacher come over yistiddy an' they had cake with jelly on top of it."

YONDER
Something that is or is in an indicted more or less distant place usually within sight (Webster came up with that one); clear?
"Yonder is whir I seen that big old 8-point buck."

YONDER WAY
That direction.
"Y'all practice your shootin' over yonder way whir they ain't nothin' but woods."

YO'NT
Do you want?
"Yo'nt to go to the pitcher show er jist ride around?"

YORE
Your.
"Gertrude got mad at Marsha fer runnin' down her young-uns, an' she told her, 'Jist mind yore own business!'"

YOUNG-UN
A human child.
"It's fine to call children *young-uns* but I don't like to hear um called *kids*, 'cause them's goats."

Overheard . . .
"Come by an' look at us." (Come and visit us.)

YOU OR PAPA ONE
Either you or Papa.
"You or Papa one come on an' eat. I got three hot cakes done ready."

YOURN
Yours.
"Jist 'cause we've been good buddies fer so long, tell you what I'll do. Since they say it's bad luck to give away a huntin' dog, you can hand me two dollars an' old Thunder Mouth will be yourn."

YOU-UNS
You people.
"You-uns shore do have a mighty perty place here."

YOU WENT BACK ON ME
An expression meaning you broke your promise to me.
"Pa, you told me you'd git me a 20-gauge when I turned twelve but you never. You went back on me an' you didn't have no cause."

ZACKLY
Exactly.
"Me'n Bruce is the same old—born on zackly the same day."

ZAT
Is that?
"Zat the same car that Fred Nugent bought from the Chivalay place brand new?"

Overheard . . .
"The dog was so lazy he had to lean against the fence to bark."